Effecting Organizational Change

And so to each new venture
Is a new beginning, a raid on the inarticulate
With shabby equipment always deteriorating
In the general mess of imprecision of feeling.

T.S. Eliot
East Coker

Effecting Organizational Change

Further Explorations of the Executive Process

Iain L. Mangham

Basil Blackwell

Copyright © Iain L. Mangham 1988

First published 1988

Basil Blackwell Ltd
108 Cowley Road, Oxford, OX4 1JF, UK

Basil Blackwell Inc.
432 Park Avenue South, Suite 1503
New York, NY 10016, USA

British Library Cataloguing in Publication Data
Mangham, Iain, *1936–*
   Effecting organizational change.
   1. Organizational change. Management aspects
   I. Title

   ISBN 0–631–15059–5

Library of Congress Cataloging in Publication Data
Mangham, Iain L.
   Effecting organizational change.

   Bibliography: p.
   Includes index.
   1.
I. Title.

   ISBN 0–631–15059–5

Typeset in 11 on 13 pt Ehrhardt
by Opus, Oxford
Printed in Great Britain by T.J. Press Ltd, Padstow, Cornwall

Contents

Acknowledgements

Among family, friends and colleagues, I especially want to thank Norman and Kevin for providing the practical support which enabled me to concentrate upon writing, Olive, Alasdair and Catriona for their forbearance as I struggled to find out what I was writing, and Joan for making sense of the manuscript. In the turmoil of what now passes for life in a university department I am, as always, grateful for the support and encouragement of my colleagues, although pressure of deadlines has meant that little of this material has been discussed with them. Finally, I must mention my good fortune in having a firm but considerate editor in Tony Sweeney.

Extracts from *Organizations as Theatre* by Iain Mangham and M. A. Overington, © 1987 John Wiley and Sons, are reprinted by permission of John Wiley and Sons Ltd. The extract from *Case Studies in Organizational Behaviour* by C. Clegg, N. Kemp and K. Legge, published in 1985 by Harper & Row, is reprinted by permission of Paul Chapman Publishing Ltd. Extracts from *The Death of Reginald Perrin*, copyright © 1975 David Nobbs, are reprinted by permission of Jonathan Clowes Ltd, London, on behalf of David Nobbs, and Victor Gollancz Ltd.

Prologue

There is a story told about a traveller who, lost in a maze of streets, stopped to ask a local the way to a particular spot. The local cogitated for a time, suggested a number of alternatives, only to dismiss each in turn before concluding: 'If I were you, I wouldn't start from here.'

In commending this book to you, I take myself to be in a similar position to that local. If I were asked to advise someone where to begin reading about the function and process of senior managers, I would suggest he or she start elsewhere. In particular, I would urge them to read not only works such as *Top Decisions*, *Decision Making at the Top* and *The Executive Mind*, but also my previous book, *Power and Performance in Organizations: An Exploration of Executive Process*.[1] Indeed, so important is this volume to the arguments advanced in the present one that I had toyed with calling this sequel, in the manner of a film, *Power and Performance II*, or *The Return of the Executive Process*.

For those unable or unwilling to follow the advice of a local, I have attempted to rehearse earlier arguments: both to begin again and resume from where I left off in the previous volume. The first chapter of the present work, with the addition of one scene, is, therefore, identical to the first chapter of *Power and Performance*. The content of much of the second chapter, with some additions and qualifications, will be familiar to readers of the first book. The additions and qualifications are important and I do not recommend short cuts. The subsequent material is new. It extends the story of the beleaguered executives portrayed in *Power and Performance* and introduces a series of ideas relating to persistence and change.

The earlier book was generally well received but a couple of issues were raised by those who either wrote about it or talked to me of it.

The first concerned the nature of the interaction depicted in the first chapter (then as now) and the second the method or style of discussion I adopted there (as here). Critics and commentators were interested that the individuals I presented appeared to spend a great deal of time considering their personal styles of interaction. A closer reading of *Power and Performance* will reveal that not to be the case; it was I rather than they who focused upon styles and patterns. In the present volume, they themselves do become more aware of the impact of their behaviour upon each other and the criticism may be more justified. I would like to emphasize, however, that this group of executives, like any other group of executives, spent most of its working day focusing upon technical matters; *my* concern was and is the interpersonal processes which are displayed in the manner in which they handle technical and task matters, and it does not follow that such a perspective informs their thoughts and actions. My emphasis has the unfortunate consequence of making these particular managers look much less competent than they were in practice. My focus is upon their difficulties, which were considerable, and upon their struggles to identify and overcome them, which were only partially successful, but this must not be taken to be a picture of their daily round. Factors such as those I am concerned with were (and are) matters of consequence, but much of an executive's time as a functional leader may be accomplished in a routine fashion; the managers who figure in these pages were as competent at that aspect of their work as any I have met, better than most. As an executive, however – a group charged with the maintenance of the organization, with the reconciling of interests and positions – they had as much difficulty as any other group, and it is this aspect that constitutes the body of this and the previous book.

The second issue is the matter of style. A number of readers quizzed me closely about the extracts: 'Where are all the false starts, the grunts and ramblings which are so much part of real life?', 'What you have to say is too rounded, too complete, too well shaped.' And so it is. In many cases, I have verbatim transcripts; in others, detailed notes written up during or immediately after the interactions. In no case is this material used direct. Literal transcriptions of tape-recorded speech may be accurate in the legal sense, may be what scholars of linguistics find fascinating to plough through, but on the page, they are lifeless. Shorn of emphasis, gesture, cadence, pitch and the like, divorced from a setting, they are indications of interaction rather than the embodiment of it. In these pages, I take my job to be to make real people, such as Paul and his colleagues, sound real. In so doing, I pick on particular words and phrases and, on occasion, give them more emphasis than they carried in real life. I provide space to describe setting and stage business, as it were, I break up long speeches, cut and shape the material, tell a story. . . .

It is, of course, a risky business. The line between fiction and this kind of reporting is not clearly drawn. I provide not all the 'facts', but a selection of them; I organize the material after the event, which gives it purpose it may well have lacked in real life. This book tells a story; like all stories, it is a matter of interpretation. To be sure, I started with the transcripts, and I actually did not invent anything, but – and it is an important 'but' – the story is selective, is patterned, is mine. I have produced a fashioning of events. What follows in these pages is not an academic report, not a scholarly disquisition upon the nature of interaction. It is an attempt to interest you in actual experiences; it is a dramatization of reality. I am in it, I have shaped it; it is of my creation. In the final analysis, it is an impression. It is the book, not the details of the interaction, which, I trust, you will find of interest.

1 Scenes from Commercial Life – Again

Afternoon: a Boardroom in the suburbs of London, late in August in the year 1983. Through a window, broken up by the slats of an expensive form of vertical Venetian blind, a panorama of chimneys, rooftops and, ant-like in the distance, a sense of urban bustle. The interior of the room is like any of a dozen such rooms – standard executive plush: large, polished, rosewood table with a number of matching chairs (comfortable yet somehow austere and business-like), thick carpeting, heavy drapes in simulated velvet covering one end of the rectangular space. The other walls are panelled in veneered rosewood, reflecting the light both from the window and from the spotlights that hang from the grid which, like some piece of stage apparatus, is suspended from the ceiling. On the table: glasses, water jugs, well cut ash trays. Writing blocks at each position; pencils neatly lined up, an expensive looking projector, propped up on a number of books. Above the head of the table, in front of the curtained wall, a large white suspended projection screen frowns down upon the assembly. There is a coffee stand, against the wall opposite the window, with three glass containers bubbling away; there are a number of cups upon it and a selection of plates and biscuits. There are two doors, each flush with the panelling, one (which leads to the toilet) almost in line with the projection machine and the other at the far end of the same wall. Midway along the wall facing the screen is a small table which has upon it, in some disarray, a number of overhead projector slides and a green telephone of a strikingly modern design.

Nine people are in the room, seated in various attitudes around the table. I am sitting at the extreme left of the table, back to the window, attempting to be of no consequence as I scribble my notes. It is a meeting of executive directors called to review results before the formal Board meeting (at which others – outsiders – will be present). At the invitation of Paul, the Managing Director, George Nisbet, the Finance Director, prepares to go through the accounts. He is a man of about fifty, of middling stature and undistinguished bearing, with a short neck and somewhat hunched shoulders, roundish head covered with greying hair, eyes hidden behind heavy spectacles, weak, almost spatulate nose but a full mouth, giving him the appearance of a somewhat belligerent baby. Dark suit, crumpled shirt, nondescript tie; dandruff on his collar. He speaks forcefully and rapidly referring both to the charts he clicks into relief upon the screen and to his notes. He avoids eye contact with his colleagues throughout his presentation and appears both embarrassed and blaming in what he has to say. He relates at some length what he terms 'the sorry saga' of 'our failure' to 'manage the business effectively'. His fellow directors, for the most part, listen, look at the projected charts, graphs and diagrams and attempt to follow what he has to say in the papers he hands out to them. None betrays any emotion or signals anything other than a minimal level of interest save Paul, who becomes increasingly and manifestly agitated . . .

George: . . . so we have failed again. For the third year we are going forward with a massive loss. I've got to say that I am ashamed. Ashamed to be associated with such figures. It seems that we, as a team, are unable or unwilling, I don't know which it is, to make the decisions that will turn this operation around. I said the same thing this time last year and we all put our hands on our hearts and swore that it would be better – and, it isn't. It's worse! We go from bad to worse . . . we don't seem to be able to come to grips with the real issues, we . . .

Paul: George, it's not worse. In a number of respects it is much better. Turn back to those charts on productivity, for example, have you got them? Look. The graph has turned up this year . . .

George: Only because we have got rid of hundreds of people; we are actually producing and selling much less than we forecast . . .

Paul: But we are producing more per employee – the trend is in the right direction and, and [*raises his voice as George seeks to interrupt*] and put up the sales graph . . . see there again the trend is upwards . . .

George: Only because we can't go lower. It's not significant, there is some movement but . . .

As George goes on to explain why things are actually as bad as he says they are, Paul becomes increasingly annoyed. He is a man in his mid forties, lean, athletic and almost completely bald. He has an assertive chin and bright, observant, blue eyes. He has discarded his jacket and rolled the sleeves of his crisp blue shirt to a position midway up his forearms. His tie is conservative and expensive, as is his suit, his watch and his pen, which he taps in irritation against his writing block, determinedly seeking to interrupt his Finance Director.

George: . . . and it's no use pointing to graphs and figures which show some upturn and claiming that as a success. That's a ridiculous way of looking at things. Christ, last month when we had a preliminary look at the figures, some of you were reporting losses of two and three million against forecast losses of four and five million and expecting a round of applause. A bloody standing ovation!

Paul: Look, George, as I am tired of telling you, against the circumstances, in the situation we find ourselves in, these figures are acceptable. The trends are in the right direction – all of the graphs point upwards. Unlike last year when things promised to be worse . . .

George: And have been.

Paul: All right. And have been. This year we are ending the year on an up turn.

George: And a thumping great loss!

Paul: I don't like the stance you are taking, George. I don't like it one little bit. I trust you are not going into next week's full Board meeting with this sort of approach . . .

George: Of course not! I know what's expected of me there! It's here and now that worries me. I find these figures totally

depressing and completely unacceptable; I am surprised
that no one else does. We all ought to resign! I mean, we
are responsible for this mess – a loss for the third year.
Seven million quid! And nobody seems to care!

The rest of the executive directors seem unperturbed by this
outburst. Some smile to themselves, others gaze fixedly out of the
window. One, Derek Morgan, the Personnel Director, rises and
crosses to the coffee table . . .

Derek: Any one for coffee?

A number respond affirmatively. He pours several cups. Alec
Barrat (responsible for a number of the factories) and Tony Gent
(in charge of another territory) look at each other and shake their
heads in a kindly, excessively tolerant fashion signalling that, like a
raging child or an incontinent lunatic, George ought to be
humoured. They have, apparently, seen it all before.

Paul: Yes, white for me. Thanks. Well, let's move on . . .

Some time later in the afternoon. A presentation is being made
by the Secretary to a small subcommittee of the executive directors
who have been considering matters of strategy. This group,
consisting of Paul, Alec Barrat, Hugh Richards (in charge of new
product development) and the Secretary (Brian Jones of the
planning department, not of director status but working directly to
Paul, the Managing Director) has been established to determine
the 'robust' decisions necessary to return the company to
profitability and to recommend these decisions to the full meeting.
A highly professional presentation is being run through with a
large number of multi-coloured charts and several overhead slides
positively bulging with figures. Most of the directors appear to be
mesmerized by the numbers and images which flit across the
screen. Few comments are made, most questions are parried with
'Well, if you don't mind we'll come to that in a minute.' Eric
Wragg, in charge of the 'after market' (until now the profitable end
of the business, charged with parts and servicing as opposed to the
supply of original equipment – the major and, at present,

unprofitable part), refuses to be deterred. He is a man of large frame and stern, even dour, presence, with thick, bushy eyebrows, strong nose, a determined mouth and a shock of barely disciplined black hair. He gives off a broad air of importance, an expectation of deference, his entire demeanour leads one to regard him as the kind of person who 'will not suffer fools gladly'. He makes his points in firm, clear tones, not without a trace, a hint, of a Midlands accent, and emphasizes each with a jabbing motion, clutching his folded spectacles in his large fist.

Eric: . . . so I don't want to wait until later. These flicker briefly and then die, but I have a nasty feeling that some of them will be resurrected at some point and it will be said that we agreed with them. What I want to know is whether or not those figures up there include the after market or not?

Brian: Which figures are you concerned about, Eric?

Eric: The ones on the far right.

Brian: These?

Eric: Yes.

Brian: Well, not directly, no. But the after market has been taken account of in our overall calculations.

Eric: I don't understand that. Either it's in those figures or it is not.

Alec: Look, you don't have to worry about it, Eric. We have taken your market into account.

Eric: Where? I can't see it. Either it's in or it is not. It makes a big difference to us as a whole. I know no one but me is interested in the non-glamorous end of the business, but we get our bread and butter from it, you know. It can't simply be ignored.

Hugh: It's not being ignored, Eric. It's in there.

Eric: Well, I can't see it and he [*indicating Brian*] cannot point to it.

Alec: We took it into account when you came to talk to us about it. You gave us the projections then and we have incorporated them.

Eric: OK. So it's in there. How much of those figures is original equipment and how much after market? Tell me that. If those people up there constitute our strategic customers it's got to be on original equipment only. There's no way that they are strategic in terms of the after market.

Hugh: We are not going to get anywhere with this. I think that we should move on.

Alec: So do I. We've been round this time and time again. Next slide.

Brian looks to Paul, as do both Hugh and Alec. He looks up the table at Eric who holds his gaze for a moment, then shrugs his shoulders, allows a thin smile to appear briefly and places his spectacles on the table. Paul nods to Brian who punches up the next chart. Alec half turns to Hugh.

Alec: [*Whispering loudly*]: I don't know why we bother to spend so much time deciding things, some clown always knows better.

Some time later. Derek is outlining his strategy for effecting 'harmonization' within the company. He has circulated a thirty page document which 'I trust you have all read', and is now going through what he terms the 'highlights'. Most of his colleagues show little interest; the interaction appears somewhat flaccid – a condition with which Derek appears to be content.

Derek: . . . so that's it, really. Quite a challenge to the way we have been doing things, but something that we have to move to.

Eric: Have to?

Derek: Have to, yes. All the indicators are that what we are proposing is best practice elsewhere and if we want to retain our employees, we must offer conditions and practices comparable with the best.

George: It will cost us dearly.

Derek: It will cost us dearly if we do not take it up.

George: But bringing everyone into line on holidays, for example, will cost an arm and a leg. Money we have not got . . .

Derek: Money we will have to find. We can't ignore trends in personnel practice. The good companies – our competitors – offer much better terms than we do.

Alec:	Has this support in the factories?
Derek:	Yes.
Alec:	Are you saying that this has the support of the people at the sharp end, those in the operating units? It's one thing for us to say OK, it's another to deliver, and they will have to deliver.
George:	And it will come as another cost to them.
Derek:	Look, it's all in the document. We have been through it – costs and everything, all laid out for you, line by line.
Alec:	And it has their support?
Derek:	Broad support, yes. Not in every detail but most of them are for it – they have to live with the people, we don't.
Alec:	Precisely.
Derek:	There is a risk, yes. It will cost money and we don't get a committed work force at the end of the day but, on balance, we take that to be a risk worth running.
Alec:	And this is the kind of thing others are doing? Competitors?
Derek:	Yes.
Tony:	Ah well, nothing ventured, nothing gained . . .

Later still. The directors are now considering the forecasts for next year which, apparently, have been passed to the Head Office in Manchester. Before each director has been placed a bulky, green-backed document, every page of which is crammed with figures. George Nisbet is once more holding forth; this time with much less aggression. Indeed he appears to be keen to skip through the text as quickly as possible, making reassuring noises to his colleagues, that what they have in front of them conforms 'very broadly to what we agreed at our last meeting'. Paul is at the green telephone – the 'hot-line' – conducting a whispered conversation with one of his superiors in Manchester. Eric is doodling upon his pad, Derek Morgan is staring fixedly out of the window and most of the others present flip through the pages with the air of men who would much rather be somewhere else. Alec Barrat, however, is clearly paying attention; indeed he has done some rapid calculations on his pad and is now reaching into his briefcase for some papers which he scans hurriedly. He is one of the younger directors – in his late thirties/early forties – shorter than average height, slightly overweight with a tense, taut bearing as though his skin were having a struggle to contain his energy. He is prodigiously fluent of speech, restless, excitable (with slightly protuberant eyes and a tendency for his emotions to be evident in his face, particularly around his mouth which, on occasions, twists rapidly into a sneer of contempt for his fellows), possibly prone to stress. A sensitive, earnest, intelligent man, quick off the mark and seen to be inclined to quarrel.

Alec: Hang on a minute, George. There's something wrong with these figures, isn't there?

George: I shouldn't think so.

Alec: Page twenty-three. Column . . . [*counts along*] One, two, three . . . seven. Forecast figures eighty four/eighty five. [*There is a scurrying of pages as most search for the relevant passage. Derek is now paying close attention, as are Eric, Hugh and Paul, who has rejoined the group.*]

George: Yes. [*A non-statement, cold, uninviting.*]

Derek: What's the problem, Alec?

Alec: Well, my copy says eleven million. Margin of eleven million.

Derek: So does mine. So what? Doesn't it tally or something? Mistake in the adding up?

Alec: [*Ignoring the questions*] How did you arrive at that figure, George?

George: The sum of columns four and six, less the numbers in five.

Alec: I can see that. I don't want the technical answer – I can do that sum for myself. It's the eleven million I'm bothered about. That wasn't the figure we agreed last time.

George: I know.

Alec: [*Consults his papers*] We agreed seventeen million.

George: Yes. [*He begins to shuffle his papers, looks towards Paul. There is a silence: it is clear that he is not going to volunteer anything further.*]

Alec: And that's what went to Manchester some [*consults his papers once more*] six weeks ago.

George: Yes.

Alec: What are these figures then?

George: Revised ones.

Alec: I can see that. Revised by whom?

George: [*Looks towards Paul who continues to avoid eye contact*] By me.

Hugh: What is the status of these figures? Does Manchester have these or the earlier ones?

George: They have these now.

There is an embarrassed silence. George gazes down at his papers. Everyone waits for someone else to break the silence, to say the unsayable.

Alec: But these are not the agreed figures.

George: [*Looking towards Paul – again no response*] They are.

Derek: What Alec is really saying, but is too polite to say, is that it is up to this group to decide what figures go forward. It's our decision and we certainly didn't agree these.

Alec: We must look a right load of idiots up in Manchester; from seventeen million down to eleven in six weeks including a three week shutdown! A barrow load of monkeys could come up with figures like that!

Eric: Got us in one! A load of monkeys.

George: The figures were revised by me and agreed with Paul. I had another look at what was being forecast and decided what had been sent up was not achievable. In fact, I didn't think eleven million was – more like four ... [*laughter and head shaking around the table*] Paul would not have that, so we sent eleven million in.

Alec: And we are supposed to be committed to that, are we?

Paul: Look, there is no point in getting excited about it. The figures don't mean anything; they will change again – they always do. We seem to be making a great fuss about nothing ...

Derek: About who decides. That's what.

George: Look, it was holiday time – you were all away. Someone had to make a decision – Christ, surely we don't have to agree everything all of the time? All of us together?

A number of separate conversations break out. The telephone whistles and Paul crosses to it, turning half towards the wall to whisper confidentially into it. Derek Morgan rises and heading towards the toilet says to no one in particular:

Derek:　What a way to run a ship!

Towards six o'clock. The meeting has been on the go for four hours. It has now reached Any Other Business. Paul is riffling through a sheaf of papers he has in front of him. A number of the directors seem anxious to leave; cases are packed and clicked noisily shut, watches are consulted, jackets are struggled into.

Paul:　One more thing. The Chairman has written a long letter explaining the change in logo.

Hugh:　The change in what?

Paul:　Logo. He has written setting out what is now to go on the top of our letters, the new colours for the envelopes, the revised packaging layouts . . .

George:　Good God! Talk about fiddling while Rome burns!

All are now giving full attention to Paul. They are on the edge of their chairs affecting almost identical expressions of incredulity at what they are hearing. A number of excited, humorous comments are passed around the table. Paul raises his voice and cuts through:

Paul:　In future, all subsidiaries of the main company including ourselves are to have the name and logo of the parent . . .

Alec:　Whom God preserve!

Paul:　. . . company placed immediately before the name of the subsidiary. Thus we shall become Twinings Friction Free Castings Ltd.

George:　We are losing millions and that's what the main Board is spending its time doing.

Eric:　What about our subsidiaries?

Paul:　What about them?

Eric:　What do they become – Twinings Friction Free Castings (LSD Camshafts) Ltd? What a bloody mouthful.

Paul: [*Consulting the letter*] It doesn't say anything about that here.

Hugh: It's probably illegal anyway.

Paul: What is?

Hugh: Changing names like that.

Eric: Certainly is – our name, our logo and our colours are registered trademarks. Cost thousands to change that.

Paul: Will it?

George: Hundreds of thousands.

Derek: What's the letter about? Asking our opinion or what?

Alec: Manchester asking our opinion? You've got to be joking!

Paul: Are you sure it will cost money to put this into effect?

Hugh: Some one up there must have taken that into account . . .

Paul: It says nothing about it here. Nothing about who is to meet the cost of changing. Lots of examples, look, all these beautiful mock-ups of what the new paper and the new packaging will look like. [*He passes out the material to willing hands.*]

Eric: Just like Christmas, isn't it?

Paul: It could well be that someone has goofed. [*Delight at this possibility is registered on most faces.*] Eric, can you take this and get someone to come up with a report on its implications – what it will cost, how much hassle it will involve us in and the like.

The meeting breaks up in rare good humour. Someone unplugs the projector, another switches the coffee machine off. Paul catches Alec's arm and steers him into a corner, engaging him in deep conversation. Most drift slowly towards the door. Expressions such as 'Bloody idiots', 'Don't know what to do with their time' and 'Fiddling while Rome burns' seem to hang on the air long after the room is vacated. I collect my belongings and, not quite knowing how to take my leave, fade away.

2 Overture and Beginners, Please

Scenes from commercial life indeed; what can be made of that kind of material? Surely, eavesdropping on conversations and stringing them together cannot be a respectable occupation for an academic, and skimming through them is of little or no value to a practitioner; at best it can produce no more than a feeling of satisfaction that people in *my* company do not behave in that fashion. What is there to learn from gossip such as this?

What is to be learned and what is to be ignored depends very much upon the model one employs to understand the phenomena with which one is confronted. In rejecting the material out of hand, in dismissing it as eavesdropping and gossip, one has recourse to an implicit model of the management process which excludes material such as I have presented in the last few pages. Willy-nilly, you have a system and are enslaved by it; all I ask is that you make heroic efforts to escape from it in order that you may consider another model, attempt to conceptualize situations such as those I depict through the use of ideas with which you may not be familiar but which you may eventually find interesting and useful.[1]

Overall, however, my framework is informed and underpinned by the school of thought referred to variously as microinteractionist, symbolic interactionist or social constructionist. However, in putting together my framework, I have drawn upon a wide range of scholars: Chris Argyris, James C. Averill, Chester Barnard, Peter Blau, Herbert Blumer, Charles Horton Cooley, Robert H. Frank, Erving Goffman, George Homans, Theodore D. Kemper, George Herbert Mead, Charles Sanders Peirce, Ted Sarbin, Richard Sennett, Robert C. Solomon, W.I. Thomas, a motley and mutinous crew of sociologists, psychologists, philosophers and economists.[2]

These writers and scholars are, in turn, heirs to patterns of thought outlined and developed years before them. This is not the time and place to attempt a history of ideas, nor am I the person to do it; however, as part of my argument is that context is important, a brief (very brief) dip into the past is necessary.

The roots of the interactionist perspective are to be found not within sociology or psychology but within philosophy, specifically that part of it called pragmatism.[3] Pragmatism, in turn, arises from idealist philosophy, which sought to effect a compromise between religion and the secular thought which emerged with the new science. Idealist philosophy pointed to the important role of consciousness in the world and even threw up notions such as Dewey's that social institutions are not objective and material but are sets of ideals by which individuals are constrained and through which they guide their conduct. Hardly revolutionary stuff from a twentieth century perspective, but pretty heady a hundred years or so ago. This led the way to even more extraordinary concepts: the individual participating in a world where he or she does not invent categories *ab initio*, but rather inherits ideas, categories and concepts in the form of language. Thus the human is not an isolated soul, an independent observer of an objective physical world which, as it were, presents him or her with categories, but an individual who participates in society and whose categorization and very thought are influenced by the language of his/her particular social group.

That's pushing idealist philosophy a bit far, to be sure, but the essence of such a view is contained within it and considerably elaborated by pragmatists such as William James and Charles Sanders Peirce[4] – particularly Charles Sanders Peirce, who was the intellectual leader of the school and a somewhat maverick one at that. His ideas are important to my position, so I will spend some time outlining them; their relevance, and that of the rest of this superficial glance at nineteenth and early twentieth century philosophy, will become clear later. Peirce's contribution was to develop a theory of the mind; he proposed that every form of thinking – deduction, induction, abduction (the term given by Peirce for the preliminary process of conjecture) – consists of some connection from one idea to another. He considered that these connnections and the laws which govern them could be

investigated logically and empirically, and founded a science –
semiotics – to do this.

Semiotics is the science of signs, and here those of you still with
me and familiar with the later work of interactionists will begin to
see links. In Peirce's view (building upon the work of the idealists
whilst rejecting the greater part of it) one never perceives or thinks
about the world directly but always through the mediation of a sign.
Meaning is always a matter of the *sign*, the *object* and the *internal
referent* or thought. As has been noted, there is no direct
connection between the idea (the internal referent) and the
external object to which it supposedly refers. The sign is always
there at the centre, exerting a controlling influence. Signs are not
isolated. They are external to the individual and they are equivalent
for everyone who uses them. Thus, words (or other symbols)
always intervene in the process of thinking and constitute an
element of the social in the individual mind.

It is rare that these signs (words, pictures or whatever) are
intrusive; Peirce conceived of mental processes as operating
unconsciously as long as the habits of inference from sign to object
are fully established and as long as nothing happens to disturb the
flow of interaction.

It is something of a step from these views to the issue of
pragmatism, but it is possible to make it without too much anxiety.
Since we cannot think without signs (and even emotions are
mediated through signs),[5] and since signs have the function of
relating us one to another, it follows that 'thinking' has a basis in
the community. What we think, that which we take to be objective,
is the product of our collective mental habits. Peirce holds that
man is simply the sum total of his thoughts, and this sum is always
a 'historical bundle' of his society's experience. We never arrive at
total certainty on anything; our working criterion of truth is 'simply
the absence of doubt, a pragmatism that is working well enough at
the time so that the ideas flow seemingly automatically'.[6]

It is an even larger step to move from these ideas to the
microinteractionist perspective as it is currently elaborated, so a
pause and an opportunity for orientation appear appropriate about
here. Interactionism (one form of the microinteractionist perspective and the one closest to my own position) views society as people
interacting with each other primarily but not exclusively through

the medium of signs and symbols. Interactionists focus upon the emergent properties of encounters and upon the processes by which individuals create and attribute meanings to people and events and the interactions which accompany them.[7]

The interactionist school is primarily a cognitive one; as I have indicated above, its emphasis is upon the human as a thinking, planning individual. I will have important qualifications to make to this model later, but for the moment I will move on to present and illustrate some glittering ideas taken from the nests of George Herbert Mead, George J. McCall and J.L. Simmons.[8]

Human beings have a capacity to manipulate signs and symbols which far exceeds those of any other species. To be sure, several types of bird can be taught to repeat words and phrases, dolphins and whales have relatively tuneful and complex patterns of communication, and apes can signal intent and mood to each other and (under special circumstances) to us. But no other creature can dream and scheme, imagine and create, philosophize and speculate, anticipate and plan, define and explain with anything approaching the skill of the least able of any one of us. Using this skill, man is a planner and a schemer; a fundamental assumption of the interactionist position is that each and every one of us wishes to make sense of that which occurs around us in order to see the implications the 'thing' has for ourselves. We may or may not have specific goals or objectives at the onset of an encounter, but once we collide with 'something' (a bundle of stimuli, in Mead's terms) then we can and do elaborate some sense of 'what does this mean for me', and meaning is closely related to plans and goals. To Paul, the 'bundle of stimuli' presented to him by George's words signals the latter's intent to screw up the Board meeting. In the light of the meaning attributed to George's words and the inference of intent he draws from them, in particular their import for his own plans (to present a united front to the Board), Paul attacks George. Like any other of us, Paul acts towards things in terms of the meaning for his existing or emergent plans of action. To be in play in any interaction, therefore, we have always to be identifying the 'things' we encounter and interpreting them to determine their meanings for our plans of action.

Thus Hugh and Alec have to monitor Eric if they are to achieve their ends; his questions about the figures have implications for their conduct as members of the inner cabinet which compiled them and must be taken into consideration in elaborating their behaviour. They must decide, at the minimum, whether to respond or not, and if so, how. This appraisal is not once for all; it is a constant activity. From that perspective, an individual may be seen to align his actions to the action or imputed action of others by assessing what he thinks their plans are; in so doing he seeks to give meaning and identity to them, himself, their acts and his own potential acts.

It may be useful at this stage to introduce one or two ideas filched from George Herbert Mead.[9] For him, all human social behaviour is built up of a continual succession of acts, each act potentially comprising four phases: impulse, perception, manipulation and consummation.

Each act begins with an impulse. An impulse is nothing more than a physiological or socially conditioned predisposition to act towards something or someone in a particular way. Again we run the danger of ascribing priority to the chicken rather than the egg, but in the example of George and Paul's interaction, the former's 'impulse' may have been to unload his sense of shame; the situation, the financial reporting session, may have 'answered to' this particular impulse. In other circumstances, the collection of people around the table may have 'answered to' an impulse to share friendship.

Perception plays a vital part in the process of the act. George has an impulse to express his shame, but his action is shaped by his perception as to what the act may look like if completed. Is this the kind of setting and circumstance in which I, George, can give vent to my feelings? Perception thus mediates between impulse and behaviour and the former may be inhibited in the light of the evaluation of the particular circumstance or situation. Whatever George's impulse to indulge in blaming behaviour, he is unlikely to enact it in the presence of strangers from Head Office (or so he claims).

Manipulation, the third phase of the act, is also a mediating phase. The financial reporting session may not turn out to be conducive to the expression of blame, shame and guilt. In our example, it is clearly not the kind of arena in which others are willing to cooperate in losing face. The value of the setting, therefore, must be reappraised and the act reorganized or redirected. George's manipulation, as I have indicated, consists in simply and dramatically continuing his castigation. Others may, at this point, have chosen to take another line. He does not, and tries to force his colleagues to 'answer to' his impulses.

Consummation is the final phase of the act. Here the impulse is satisfied (or not). In George's case, it is clearly not satisfied if it is assumed, as I have to now, that he wishes to unload his sense of shame. If, on the other hand, George's impulse is to provoke Paul and/or to provide I-told-you-so opportunities for the future, then his act is splendidly consummated. Success, however, cannot be guaranteed and there is, potentially, many a slip between impulse and consummation.

It is clear, or should be, that social acts are effected through symbols. Through the medium of language, each of us calls particular responses from others or attempts to call them forth. Words such as 'failed again', 'ashamed', 'ridiculous', 'depressing' and 'unacceptable', phrases such as 'nobody seems to care', are provocative. It is possible that all of us in the room perceived them in a similar fashion, but, aside from Paul, since none of us responded by being provoked, we denied George his perverse satisfaction. Severally the 'impulses' we each experienced may or may not have been inhibited or satisfied by the circumstance of George's strictures. In my case, George's outburst 'answered to' my impulse to collect data and record it for future use. In Derek's case, Alec's or Tony's, an 'impulse' not to become involved may have been consummated without the need for manipulation.

What is important to recognize is that each of these acts is interdependent and, ultimately, interlocked. Had George succeeded in provoking others into expressions of shame (assuming that were his 'impulse', his intent), then the pattern would be clear and consummation obvious. Nonetheless, even his failure may be seen as part of a process; his enactment of his impulse leads to a response, even if this is not the kind of response he had perceived or sought to manipulate; this response (or to complicate matters even more, these responses) becomes part of the data he must process to continue the interaction; his response to our response becomes part of our further enactments; and so on.

The means by which this alignment occurs are well presented by George McCall and J.L. Simmons.[10] Essentially, we are able to interact as we do because of our capacity to manipulate symbols and our ability to dream, plan, fantasize and imagine. Weber expresses the notion I am seeking to depict as the ability each of us possesses 'to put oneself imaginatively in the place of the actor and thus sympathetically to participate in his experience' and Shibutani declares that imaginative participation or 'role taking' consists of 'anticipating what another human being is likely to do [which] requires getting "inside" of him – to his objective experiences, his particular definition of the situation, and his conception of his own place within it'.[11] Imaginative participation or role taking, which interactionists hold to be a fundamental human attribute, may be defined as the ability to put oneself in the place of others through the use of the imagination, to see things with their eyes and on the basis of these imaginings (for that is what they are) to predict how they will react. Hugh anticipates that Eric will continue to 'make trouble' whatever clarification is offered; thus he frames his conversation and his interaction with that predominant assumption.

George Herbert Mead, who was much exercised by the notion of role taking, pointed out that 'taking the role of the other' can mean imaginatively participating in the life of a specific person in a specific interaction or incorporating into one's own actions what one takes to be the view of a wider grouping – the 'generalized other'. Hugh's and Alec's dealings with Eric, therefore, are informed not only by that which they imagine to be the likely responses of the latter to their blandishments, but also, in part, by views they have formed about the likely reactions of others to their manner of dealing with him. They feel free to ignore his questions and even to pass open comment upon his actions, since they believe, not erroneously as it turns out, that Eric will receive no support from his colleagues. The context appears to be one in which both Alec and Hugh feel free to treat a colleague as 'awkward'. One can imagine other contexts in which such comments were either more frank (open, not whispered), challenged or not allowable in any form.

So, summarizing so far, I have depicted a process in which two or more individuals come together to accomplish some joint act.

The beginnings of such an endeavour consist of one party offering a definition of what he takes to be the appropriate conduct for the prosecution of the encounter. Eric decides to ask some questions. Brian is clearly willing to answer, Alec less so. He, by a process of self-interaction, clearly comes to the conclusion that Eric is not merely seeking information (given the challenging tone of Eric's first intervention, this may hardly seem surprising). Putting himself imaginatively into Eric's shoes, he does not like what he sees developing, particularly for his own part in the interaction. Alec does not wish to be placed in the role of one being interrogated. He may well feel that such a process once embarked upon threatens all kinds of valued self-identities (as a member of the strategic group, he is privy to information which, whilst restricted, makes him special) and he may, therefore, mentally rehearse courses of action which deny Eric the purpose he attributes to him. Thus the cognitive processes of self-interaction and role taking (which may continue throughout the interaction) have 'to do with judging the identities that the various interactors . . . are likely to claim in the situation'.

As this quote illustrates, in *The Presentation of Self in Everyday Life* Erving Goffman sets out to describe and understand the ways in which an individual lays claim to a particular identity in an encounter.[12] Interaction, for Goffman, is frequently 'strategic'; consequently a great deal of effort goes into controlling the impression one gives in order to direct the action along lines conducive to one's own ideas (planned or emergent). Goffman makes a distinction between two classes of expression; those that are 'given' and those that are 'given off':

> The first involves verbal symbols or their substitutes which he uses admittedly and solely to convey the information that he and others are known to attach to these symbols. This is a communication in the traditional and narrow sense. The second involves a wide range of action that others can treat as symptomatic of the actor, the expectation being that the action was performed for reasons other than the information conveyed in this way.[13]

Thus individuals by carefully controlling their expressive behaviours can convey to other individuals – by impressions given and given off – an image of who it is they wish to be taken for in a particular encounter. In so doing they attempt to constrain those others to accept their claims. Eric knows what he is about when he asks his questions and his choice of mild aggression rather than soft request is an attempt to set the interaction off along lines he favours: the colleague asserting his right to know. Of course, should the impression that Eric gives off be less than congruent with the impression that he attempts to give – let us say he questions in a tremulous tone, with a markedly nervous twitch – it may be that his attempts to constrain will be even less successful. Alec and Hugh may respond to the weakness they impute to Eric rather than to the dominance which the latter seeks to impose upon the interaction. One's conduct must be of a piece if one's claim to leverage in a particular encounter or interaction is to be sustained.

The obverse of self-presentation is the notion of altercasting:

In interaction the participants project identities for themselves and for each other. Not only do they present a particular image of self but they also cast the alter in the position that they would like him to assume.[14]

Eric's assumption of a questioning stance conveys to others that they should assume the roles of information suppliers. A claim to dominance in an interaction simultaneously and necessarily casts others into submissive postures; a claim to weakness is equally an attempt to cast others into the position of strength. In other words, identities may be seen as reciprocal; what Eric does constrains his colleagues, and their responses, theoretically at least, in turn constrain Eric. However, it is important to note that neither presentation of self nor altercasting automatically brings into line the roles and identities that individuals party to an encounter wish to enact. The processes outlined above do not structure encounters on a once for all basis; whatever Eric offers or asserts may be accepted or challenged by his colleagues. In many encounters competing definitions emerge and, should all concerned wish to continue the interaction, such definitions must be taken into account. It is usual to note a degree of negotiation in encounters:

Typically the two parties will negotiate some sort of
compromise, each acceding somewhat to the other's
demands, though seldom in equal degree ... this compromise definition of the role and character of each is not
executed in a single step but is the eventual result of a
complex process of negotiation or bargaining.[15]

It is important to stress once more the emergent quality of much
interaction. Interactionism, of course, assumes that human beings
are purposeful creatures, actively seeking to define and sustain
their objectives, and further assumes that the result of people
coming together is a negotiation, a compromise; joint actions have
an emergent quality 'that may not have existed before the parties
came together'. The fitting together of individual lines of action
provides the basic feature of joint action which, in and of itself, is
more than happenstance. It can be seen as a cognitive process of
combining separate, partial and sometimes conflicting definitions
and competing claims to identity into a meaningful if temporary
relation. It is temporary since the emergent quality of such
'working agreements' makes their attainment problematic and their
course potentially unstable.[16] There are essentially two stages to
the attainment of a negotiated agreement. The first is the
negotiation of social identities – who is being who in this
encounter: 'Me Tarzan, you Jane'. The second is the negotiation
of interactive roles, the agreement on the specifics of the
interaction – what is to be done and by whom. The working
agreement is thus a delicate balance of identities and tasks; should
anyone object to the identity imputed to him, the subsequent joint
action may well be of a different character or it may totally break
down.

To return to my colleagues waiting in the Boardroom. How do
they arrive at a working agreement? I shall focus in particular on
the fourth extract in chapter 1, the one in which George presents
the figures that he has sent up to Manchester. In non-routine
interactions such as this, the first problem is one of definition. The
identities, roles and goals which each is accustomed to using no
longer seem appropriate; individualistic approaches to such
meetings where, by and large, the best course of action has been to
'defend your own patch' or somewhat more aggressively to 'kick

over the milk bottles on someone else's step before they kick over yours', do not seem the most appropriate response to the developing situation. It could well be that for a time, at least, each is unclear as to how to proceed. As Alec continues to probe, however, it becomes clear to one or two that he may well need support. Eric, for example, may know this but may well be unable to think of himself as a 'supporter' of Alec, even less so given their previous interactions. Even were he to conceive of such an identity, it may be that he could not play it with conviction. In any event, he may not be able to define the goal. Is the developing purpose to 'screw George'? If so, at least that sort of line is familiar. Or is it, as Derek seems to imagine, to assert the authority of the group? And if so, what is Paul's reaction likely to be? What does his silence, his avoidance of support for George, mean? Is he punishing him for the previous encounter or is something else afoot?

To most of my executives this is a relatively new situation, and their hesitations, their inability to define identities and roles for themselves and others, are products of inexperience and unfamiliarity. Those concerned must cast around in an attempt to define what is going on and what is to be their part in it. Given the lack of definition, there are a number of options open to the actors. The most frequently observed is withdrawal. Hugh and Eric appear to prefer this course of action, saying little and sitting back from the table. Alec, however, characteristically prefers to edge forward, seeking to find what kind of circumstance he is facing: 'Well, my copy says eleven million. Margin of eleven million.' Derek, at this stage unclear as to what is going on but, perhaps, sensing something odd, something untoward in George's manner of response, seeks to understand Alec's point. Alec, either intent upon his own line or unwilling (perhaps unable) to develop a different kind of relationship with Derek, simply continues: 'How did you arrive at that figure, George?'; he does not want a literal answer but gets one, either because George fails to understand his intent or, more likely given the hostility in his tone, because he perceives the intent and chooses to ignore it. Alec takes another tentative step, George's tone and manner acting as a goad: 'I can see that.' If, as appears to be the case, George wishes to shut off the inquiry, his self-presentation is unfortunate since it is such as to further it. He clearly has not got his act together. Alec moves on:

'We agreed seventeen million.' The intent of his statement is 'Explain yourself, George. Explain yourself.' George simply says 'Yes.' Alec's challenge is ambiguous enough for him not to have to respond. If he wants an answer, he must be much more direct, which he gradually becomes: 'Revised by whom?' George once more looks towards Paul who continues to ignore him. Such behaviour is likely to have entered into Alec's definition of the situation, and hence he proceeds with caution: something is up, but who is involved? Is this me against George or me against George and Paul? If the latter, the consequences are likely to be different. But Paul is not supporting him. Why not? Because he knows nothing about the circumstance? Hugh, who has sat back for a while, thinks he has discovered what the interaction is about and has hit upon an identity and role for himself. He is less concerned about his relationship with Paul than is Alec, and has fewer problems with Alec than does Derek; he can therefore support him and essay a direct question: 'Does Manchester have these [figures] or the earlier ones?' The answer stops everyone in his tracks. Each reflects upon its meaning. The situation has now changed from one of exploring to one of considering the implications of what has now been revealed. Again, for most, withdrawal appears to be the best course of action. Alec, however, proceeds. Again, by indirection he seeks to find direction out: 'But these are not the agreed figures.' George denies the premise and Derek, seeking to support Alec, directly confronts the issue: 'It's our decision and we certainly didn't agree these.' The pattern of interaction is rapidly developing into one of group versus George (and, possibly, Paul). However, Alec does not build upon Derek's dramatic outlining of the issue. Either he does not perceive it or he does not welcome Derek's support (it is not within his repertoire to handle support from that source). In any event, George's goading promotes an angry outburst which temporarily deflects Derek's purpose and leads to Eric's quite inappropriate attempt at joking: 'Got us in one! A load of monkeys.' No one laughs, Eric withdraws once more. George is stung into a response by the tone of both Alec's and Eric's comments which he appears to read as dismissive and contemptuous. In responding, he associates Paul with his actions, thus overtly confirming his earlier signals. It is now too late for Alec to withdraw and he proceeds until interrupted by Paul who, responding to the obvious acrimony, seeks to downplay the event: 'Look, there is no point in getting excited about it.' The interaction splutters to a halt, finally sealed off by Derek's exit line – 'What a way to run a ship!' Although all concerned collude in the termination of this particular scene, the issue of who decides does not appear to be resolved. It is, of course, actually resolved since, by not pursuing the issue further, Alec, Hugh and Derek leave the decision where it was before they raised the matter – in the hands of George and Paul.

Although the episode seems to peter out, it nonetheless furnishes me with one example of what may be termed 'negotiating order'.[17] It has the hallmarks of a negotiation: there are divergent definitions of the situation, there is also the possibility of compromise (although it may not appear so), those involved operate tentatively and provisionally (particularly Alec), and until quite late in the event there is the possibility that no imposed solution will be forthcoming (Paul remains silent, enigmatic). Looked at in these terms, Alec defines the situation, explores his definition, observes and considers reactions to this exploration, moves ahead in the light of his view of likely reactions and repeats the cycle. George observes Alec's intent and decides whether or not to offer concessions. As I have shown, he offers none, but has to reconsider as the encounter develops and is eventually driven to justifying himself and his actions. A compromise is offered: look, lads, it was a matter of holidays, no one to turn to and so forth. This is not offered in a manner likely to win friends and influence people, but, significantly, George does feel the need to justify his actions. This is a step which may be satisfactory to Alec and Hugh, possibly even to Derek. The person they see as usually dogmatic and inflexible has been forced to give and, even more worthwhile, we who pushed him into this do not need to accept his compromise. We have the moral victory.

This perspective implies that Alec and his colleagues 'win' and George loses; they allow the encounter to conclude in the manner that is due with Derek having the triumphant exit line. It is possible, however, to see the conclusion in quite another light. The rewards to Alec of pursuing George are such that – at each stage save the last – it is worth the chase. The costs that he has to bear are those of George's hostility. He is 'safe' until Paul, his composure temporarily and successfully disturbed by George's stonewalling, is drawn in when the circumstances clearly change. The costs of annoying Paul are likely to be much higher, the rewards much less tangible. Paul's power to punish is such as to make even the most subtle of warnings an implicit threat: 'We seem to be making a great fuss about nothing.' Paul is the key actor in most of the interactions, becoming more so with every word he fails to utter. Once he has spoken, given his command over both rewards and punishment, his definition becomes one that must be and is taken into consideration.

Such a course of events is, of course, unusual. However logical the exposition may appear, you and I know that the occasions when we behave in anything like the fashion sketched out in these pages are few and far between. Only exceptionally are we *conscious* of a process of interpretation, planning, negotiating and behaving; more often than not we simply behave.

We are not alone in our doubts. Peirce, anticipating Freud and many others by a score or so years, conceived of the mental processes – the means by which we know what is appropriate behaviour and effect such behaviour – as operating unconsciously as long as the behaviour is routine and firmly established and nothing happens to disturb the processes of definition and action.[18] Much of our everyday interaction is routine and predictable, much of it simply re-creates and maintains well established patterns of behaviour. Such routines have been termed 'scripts'. There are scripts for entering a restaurant, for going to the bank, for dating a partner, for conducting meetings at the office, for routine interaction virtually anywhere.[19]

In the first extract in chapter 1, George's behaviour, however odd it may appear to us, is as familiar to his colleagues as is Paul's response to it. George is seen to be 'doing his Cassandra bit', forecasting gloom and doom and claiming to feel bad about it, and Paul challenges and reassures him. George characteristically sees the bad side of events, Paul seeks to emphasize the good. The others say little and appear to be uninvolved with the proceedings although they, collectively, are being castigated by George. To an outsider, this appears to be a highly dramatic event, one in which the conspiracy of silence around poor operating results is broken. The response culminating in 'Anyone for coffee?' is surprising.

Not so to the participants, however. For them, it seems the situation is routine, something with which they are familiar. They can and do readily name the interaction 'George-doing-his-Cassandra-bit'. They appear to know the rough shape of the interaction: George will 'sound off', Paul will become 'irritated', George will continue, will be interrupted and 'corrected', will modify his stance somewhat and – barring accidents – the 'outburst' will be contained. The roles, including that of the spectators (whose role in this interaction is to sit and stare impassively), appear to be well known and well rehearsed. The pattern of activities that will occur is broadly known and it strongly resembles those that have taken place on similar occasions. 'We have seen it all before.' In such circumstances, those concerned, Paul, George and the others, can and do perform with relatively little effort; once triggered, the routine script is run off automatically.

Here is another example of a script. This time it is Tony Gent (one of the general managers), whom we discover drinking coffee and developing his ideas:

Tony: Quite straightforward really. The Brazilians are in the market for agricultural equipment, we've got it, they want it, so I can see no reason for holding back.

Alec: I can. The machinery they want is obsolescent, we are winding down on production of U 40s, there is no market for them . . .

Tony: Correction. There is. Brazil.

Alec: Yes. Brazil, and only Brazil.

Tony: It's a very big market, Alec. A vast opportunity providing we get in there quickly.

Alec: It's not that simple. If, and I stress *if*, we were to go in for that we need to keep open the plant at Chesterfield which we have just resolved to close – can the Brazilians bear the cost of that?

Tony: With great respect, Alec, that is not their concern. It may be ours but it is not theirs. They want U 40s, we have them. If we respond within six weeks, we have a market. If not, not.

Alec: We cannot possibly respond on a timetable as tight as that. Brazil is no part of our strategic plan, neither are U 40s, for that matter, except to phase them out.

Tony: Plans are made to be changed, Alec, opportunities are there to be sought. [*Looks towards Paul*]

Paul: This does appear to be worth looking at.

Again, insiders and observers (after a time) can recognize this particular pattern. Tony-doing-his-reasonable-man bit, the market opportunity which is there provided a quick response is forthcoming. In my time observing the group interact, he performed this role on four occasions, each time presenting his colleagues either with an opportunity which 'demanded' a quick response or a crisis which 'required' instant resolution. He did so in his careful, polite and what I took to be a down-putting manner, and on every occasion was opposed by Alec and on every occasion successfully brought Paul into the conversation on his side. I doubt whether any of this was planned, any of it was thought out, it was a characteristic way of these particular actors performing. They did not set out to irritate Alec, nor did Alec set out to attack Tony. Both dance to the music of their time, neither conscious as they do it of their steps or of the patterns they describe.

Nonetheless, scripts are the products of people as information processors; a fundamental assumption of my approach to the description and analysis of behaviour in organizations is that people *can* become engaged in attempts to understand and control what is happening around them. This is not to assert that all of us (or any of us at some particular moment) are conscious seekers of information: that is rarely the case. However, in ideal terms each of us can (and occasionally does) engage in a process of ascribing meaning to, or imposing meaning upon, experience and each of us can use meanings so derived as the basis for action. Scripts may be regarded as examples of mindless behaviour, rule or schema based behaviour, which prove the exception. They serve to illustrate that none of us deals rationally with each and every piece of information *each* time we confront it; scripts illustrate a form of cognitive economy in which behaviour is run off with little or no reflection and virtually no effort. This should not blind us to the fact that all scripts were once – long ago and far away – a matter of cognitive effort and may become so again given a change in circumstances.

I will work through the interaction between George and Paul to illustrate the script concept. Neither of our heroes approaches events with an open mind; each 'knows' how to behave in circumstances such as this one. The situation is not unclear nor is it ambiguous: the presentation of results is a cue, a trigger for a pattern of automatic or 'mindless' behaviour to be invoked. Both George and Paul have built up a repertoire of tacit knowledge that is used to impose structure and meaning upon events such as the meeting in the Boardroom. They have actually and metaphorically been here before, each has experienced what they take to be similar events many times before; in schematic form, each knows his part and that of the other. Little mutual effort is required for the performance to be convincing and satisfying. So used are these particular performers to each other and the situation that they may no longer pay attention to what is being said; meaning construction for each of them involves association of this experience with previous experiences. As Walter Lippman put it many years ago, 'For the most part, we do not see first and then define. We define first and then see.'[20] It takes but the simplest of cues to provoke the scene.

Episodes such as those occurring between George and Paul, Alec and Tony, are matters of considerable consequence since they reflect and encapsulate 'understandings' of how people within Friction Free Castings should behave. If any one of the actors were to be asked how should they act in financial reporting meetings or strategy discussions, it is unlikely that they would give a step by step outline of events. It is much more probable that they would refer to their symbolic or metaphorical understanding of the events: George-doing-his-Cassandra-bit, Paul-smoothing-over-problems, Tony-putting-Alec-down, Tony-getting-away-with-murder, Tony-and-Alec-battling-it-out-again. These symbolic or metaphorical assertions are more than descriptions; they channel perceptions and influence behaviour. Once I can label a particular interaction as an example of Paul smoothing or whatever, I am home and dry, I need do nothing more than participate in line with the demands of that particular script. George-doing-his-Cassandra-bit allows me to sit back and ignore him. My experience and that of some of my colleagues has been that refusing to be roused by George's strictures, refusing to feel 'shame' and 'guilt'. and signalling that refusal through a studied indifference, has consequences which are, by and large, rewarding. George will not physically attack anyone, he will not storm out and present me with a potentially embarrassing circumstance, nor will he go on for ever. Eventually he will fizzle out, having provoked Paul to intervene. His behaviour and that of Paul makes sense in so far as it fits in with my symbolic representation of it and in so far as it follows a pattern which fits this representation. Should George leap upon the table and break into a Fred Astaire routine with Paul or, equally bizarre given what we expect of him in events such as this, should he begin to praise himself and his colleagues, the event would be rendered prob-lematic and we would all have to do some rapid cognitive work to find an appropriate script for handling it. That redefinition would have consequences: 'he-is-pissed-out-of-his-mind' would imply different action from us than would the definition 'this-is-a-technique-for-grabbing-attention-he-learned-on-a-course-last-week'.[21]

My argument is simple, the implications of it immense. Most of us, most of the time, in most circumstances, at home, work or play, perform without reflection. Even in circumstances where we are theoretically called upon to reflect – planning meetings, interviews, decision points in our life and the like – most of us tend to enact our parts in well established scripts.

Most of us, most of the time, in most circumstances, act consistently in that if we were to observe ourselves on film, we would see that – for the most part – what we do and say in any one scene resembles what we do and say in preceding and successive scenes: most of our performances echo and re-create familiar patterns, and whatever novelty we do demonstrate is but a variation on a theme rather than a significant departure from it.

Most of us, most of the time, in most circumstances, do not behave in line with a set of goals and intentions; our behaviour is not consciously strategic. Contrary to the explicit model of cognitive theorists and management consultants, we rarely make conscious decisions that determine our actions. We do not consciously define situations, consider implications of those definitions, elaborate alternative responses, test them, select one and behave. We simply behave. Our behaviour frequently lacks intent and is manifestly bereft of motive. 'Gentlemen, shall we begin?' is sufficient to trigger us into a couple of hours of patterned behaviour.

The behaviour may be mindless, but is not pointless. Scripts are great conservers of energy. When social actors are cued into set routines – which happens most of the time – they do not expend time and effort discovering appropriate actions all over again; they simply 'perform' – bring to fruition – a familiar script. George-doing-his-Cassandra-bit cues most of the executives into patterns of indifference and saves each of them the effort of elaborating any other response to him. Similarly, though less obviously, Paul *knows* how to behave, certain words and phrases – 'shame', 'failure' – cue him, and he performs his by now well known routine of it's-much-better-than-you-claim. Such scripts demand little or no reflection on the part of any of those involved and they produce actions and feelings very much like those which have obtained in what we take to be similar circumstances in the past.

Such scripts account for almost all behaviour in organizations. Thirty-odd years ago, March and Simon were making the same point:

> Situations in which a relatively simple stimulus triggers off an elaborate program [script] of activity without any apparent interval of search, problem-solving, or choice are not rare. They account for a very large part of the behavior of all persons, and for almost all of the behavior of persons in relatively routine positions. Most behavior, and particularly most behavior in organizations, is governed by performance programs.'[22]

I don't like the terminology – 'program' has a mechanistic quality which denies the improvised quality of human interaction – but I cannot but agree with the sentiment. We learn our scripts through a variety of means: at mother's knee, from school, the media, company indoctrinations, precedents, rituals and traditions, and we cope with situations by applying our learning with little or no reflection.

Organizations such as Friction Free Castings cash in upon the human propensity to enact scripts by creating cues which trigger responses without the need for any reflection at all upon the part of the participants. George talks about the figures at this particular meeting because he has always talked about the figures fifteen days after the end of the month; that is when they are collated and made available for discussion. That is when the agenda of the meeting begins with 'Discussion of results'.

Friction Free Castings is full of such scripts, triggered not by a particular need to address production targets, financial results, market reports, prices, management development or whatever, but by routine assignments and the calendar. As has been pointed out elsewhere,[23] even if scripts were first elaborated to meet specific needs, they soon become self-generating when those responsible for their enactment are given budgets and assigned offices; Friction Free Castings has open days, outings for pensioners, long-service dinners, sports days, and recruitment fairs, not because such events meet any particular needs of the organization, but because some part of the bureaucracy enacts them and no one asks why.

The strength of such behaviour lies in the fact that it saves us all a great deal of effort. If I had to pay attention to everything in which I were involved, the cognitive stress would be considerable; it would probably be disabling. Scripts, the following of routines, theoretically should free me to concentrate upon those facets of interaction and experience which are matters of consequence. Routines should provide me with time, space and energy to deal with important issues. Unfortunately, this is rarely the case since what constitutes an important issue is frequently determined by a particular script and the process of reflection is itself routinized.

To illustrate what I mean, let us, once more, return to dear old George and Paul. They are talking about the figures and they are talking about them (a) because received wisdom says that organizations should set goals and should record progress and the stock market expects it of them, (b) because managerial ideology as inculcated by the media, by business schools, by other managers, says they should regularly discuss results, and (c) because George's department regularly and routinely gathers data, collates it and pushes out a report such as that currently in front of them.

What is collected is a matter of routine; what is provided is a series of figures about output, stock turnover, sales, cash position and so on, together with an assessment of why things are as they are seen to be from the figures and what the manager responsible is doing to rectify matters (where rectification is taken to be appropriate). It does not produce, for example, routine data on the costs of new product development, or anything on the training and development expenditure, and it never seeks to investigate whether expenditure on capital projects meets the returns outlined in the original justification of these products. Thus what the executive of Friction Free Castings is invited to pay attention to is limited by the kinds of data presented and biased by the problem definitions and solutions proposed by the general managers (some of whom are sitting round the table). Furthermore, as I have illustrated, the process of reflecting is scripted: George will seek to make the rest feel bad and Paul will deny him the opportunity – the rest will remain silent. On the few occasions that this does not occur, the members of the executive will reflect upon the figures in a predictable and relatively routine fashion. Poor figures – such as the ones under consideration – will lead to talk of cutting costs, controlling headcount ('no recruitment without the managing director's signature'), and similar short term approaches. Reflection at Friction Free Castings consists in *not* thinking radically, *not* raising fundamental issues about the market and their place in it. As the problems increase, the denial script may become less tenable and some radical postures may be adopted, but they are (and in this case were) softened by the routine which demanded that more facts were needed before any radical action could be undertaken. Procrastination dressed up as analysis is a common pattern in many organizations.[24]

Paul is not alone in accentuating the positive, although he is probably unique in accepting the data in front of him as confirming his expectations. Although it is fragmented, his team remains ready to attribute good results to their own actions and blame bad results on factors beyond their control: the market, suppliers, the rail strike, customers, the unions or whatever. Consequently, bad results do not elicit action. Indeed, they are best ignored: 'these figures are acceptable. The trends are in the right direction – all of the graphs point upwards.'

In the sequence in which they agree to Derek's proposals concerning the 'harmonization' of employment policies, the script-like quality of reflection and decision making is equally obvious. Derek begins the session with but the briefest outline of the background which no one subsequently challenges or questions. His presentation assumes a widespread acceptance of the problem as he defines it (in turn conditioned by the kind of data routinely collected by the Personnel Department) and implies even in the definition of the issue the necessary action to resolve it. Derek may be convinced of his solution and may look for support from his colleagues, but he cannot and does not seriously expect it. In this organization, as in many others, the script is such that no one will seek clarification, or even a detailed description, of the circumstance which requires resolution, but nor will they give unequivocal support to a solution.

To be sure, those around the table 'go along' with Derek's ideas, but they do so in a manner which both he and they know is non-committal. Some of them ask questions, some declare a lukewarm enthusiasm, but most call upon well worn phrases and sayings to move the decision making along. Alec, for example, quizzes Derek, but in a fashion which avoids confronting any matter of fundamental importance about the proposal: 'Are you saying that this has the support of the people at the sharp end, those in the operating units?' And again: 'And this is the kind of thing others are doing?' This has the effect of distancing Alec from whatever decision eventually emerges: others who ought to know better than me support this, or so Derek claims, and other companies apparently are moving this way. He does not have to give up his role of interrogator, nor does he, personally, have to display commitment to the move towards harmonization. If it fails, those fools down the organization or elsewhere are to blame, or you, Hugh, for having misinterpreted their views, not me.

Tony's comments are also interesting in that they are vacuous, empty of matter. They reflect an apparent vacancy of mind around the issue of harmonization, but serve also to signal endorsement of but not commitment to the subject under discussion. 'Nothing ventured, nothing gained' is a tired, well worn phrase, but picks up on what Tony takes to be the underlying import of Derek's proposal: that there is an element of risk. The value of such a cliché lies in its very lack of originality, its apparent emptiness.[25] Tony's statement does not directly challenge Hugh, does not invite him to spell out the downside of his proposals; instead it floats in the air, offered but not taken up, inane and pregnant with meaning at one and the same time.

What is going on here, of course, is not just a matter of edging into a decision. To be sure, the rephrasing and the clichés signal a level of agreement, but it is, at best, tentative. It certainly seems to distance the speakers from the proposer. Those who grunt, vaguely nod or stare into space are even less committal. The process is enacted, however, to secure commitment, however weak. Members of Friction Free Castings, and of other teams, are unhappy if only one or two people overtly agree to a course of action. They are equally unhappy if everyone wants to contribute: 'I don't know why we bother to spend so much time deciding things, some clown always knows better.' Clichés and rephrasings enable a number of people to go through the motions of agreeing without disturbing anyone too much. It is the minimum level of cooperation and little more is expected or required. Sharp interrogation of the person who talks in clichés, examination of he who rephrases, threatens the fragile thread of pseudo-communication and is often not undertaken.[26]

There are, of course, circumstances in which routine breaks down – ones in which the performers are not clear what to do. Alec's questioning of the figures has a tentativeness about it which is unusual for this group and alerts us to the fact that something out of the ordinary is unfolding. Social actors can become aware of their circumstances, particularly when encountering a novel situation, but also when performing a particular script becomes effortful, when others depart from it or interrupt it and when the setting does not allow for sufficient involvement. Who-sent-the-figures is a novel circumstance which causes those concerned to cast around for a way of handling the circumstance. The other points are less easy to illustrate directly; I can do no more than offer hypothetical examples. Assume that George literally had to stand up and shout about 'shame', 'failure' and the like; in such a circumstance, the effort required may make him aware of the nature of his behaviour. Similarly, if others were to interrupt him half-way through his first sentence and ask him whether or not he needed a tranquillizer or a chance to lie down, this too might cause him to become aware of his script. Equally, George trying to do his

Cassandra bit at the annual Christmas party may bring him to realize how inappropriate and ineffective his usual line is.

Such awareness, however, rarely lasts a long time. Where scripts are found wanting, social actors cast around to find other apparently more appropriate scripts and hurriedly call them up. Only in the most exceptional of circumstances are executives (or any one else, for that matter) willing to live with the kind of ambiguity which arises from the absence of a script.

'We don't manage too badly, eh Didi, between the two of us? We always find something, eh Didi, to give us the impression that we exist.[27]

I will have more to say about interruption of routines and novel circumstances later. However, before doing so I want to introduce the notion of improvisation into my argument and illustrate it from the transcripts. I wish to put forward the radical notion that all we observe at Friction Free Castings, or elsewhere, is interaction around a couple of basic referents.

In what I take to be novel or problematic circumstances, it is clear that I am involved in a process somewhat different to that which I experience in ones which I take to be routine interactions. What the notion of improvisation implies is that we are each capable of performing along a continuum from 'pure' information (the apparent absence of any referent for our behaviour) to classic theatre (the circumstance where every word and utterance is composed for us). In fact, neither extreme is reached in practice since no one of us can avoid the use of previously learned material and no classical performer can repeat his or her performance without some variations, however minute. Nonetheless, when I experience 'things' which I cannot quickly label (link to a referent), I am conscious of a different manner of enactment to that which occurs in more familiar circumstances. On occasion, it takes but a little time to 'discover' the referent and I am soon on familiar ground; on other occasions, I and my colleagues cast around for a while before we find common ground and can interact with our accustomed fluency.

Perhaps the best way of indicating what I mean by a referent is by taking an example from music and another from theatre.[28] The simplest pattern of improvisation in music is that in which a given melody is the referent and some aspects of it are changed whilst others essential to the preservation of its identity are maintained. Stereotyped ornamentation formulas (which in turn can become referents) typically develop alongside free embellishments. In such a circumstance, however, we can hear the referent throughout most of the piece and it influences the improvisation, although it may be antagonistic or contrapuntal rather than direct and imitative.

In the theatre, the best known form of improvised theatre is the Commedia dell'Arte, which I have commented upon extensively elsewhere.[29] In this type of playing, it is primarily the characters who serve as the referent for the subsequent improvisation; there is a plot but it is simple and often somewhat thin. The essential fact about the Commedia is that each troupe consisted of a constellation of characters who remained the same, regardless of the plot they found themselves embroiled in. The modern-day equivalent would be the Marx brothers; add their customary accomplice or butt, the well endowed Margaret Dumont, and one or two bit players and there it is, a comedy based upon comic strip characters. Wherever they found themselves, at the races, the circus or the opera, they remained essentially the same.

This referent for improvisation, of course, can be applied to our heroes. The characters that George and Paul, Alec, Hugh and Eric perform may be seen as unchanging and stereotypical: George is always doing his sackcloth and ashes bit, Paul his positive but somewhat heavy handed paternal bit, Alec his sharp, combative manager, and so on. Given what they know of each other, what they expect of each other, what they cast each other into, we could well regard the 'characters' of these performers as being the primary referent for their improvisations. It is a potentially interesting line, but not one which I intend to pursue since I believe there is more, much more, to interactions such as these in this or any other organization.

The referents for a great deal of what occurs at Friction Free Castings (as elsewhere) are primarily *authority* and *fraternity*. Indeed, I will go as far as declaring that there is nothing else to observe in these or any other kind of interactions than technical activities and improvisations around issues of authority and fraternity.

This is by no means a new idea, although my terms may differ from those used by others. A large number of studies of the variables of interpersonal behaviour (what I refer to here as the referents of behaviour) have come to the conclusion that major portions of the interactions in which we daily engage can profitably and reasonably accurately be conceived of as involving variations on two independent, bipolar dimensions.[30] One of these may be termed the *power* dimension, a continuum with dominance at one extreme of it and submission at the other; and the other, *love*, with love at one extreme and hate at the other. Along the first dimension would be ranked assertive, managing, leading, controlling, retiring, consenting, obsequious and following behaviours; along the second, loving, accepting, affectionate, friendly, attracting, aggressive, rejecting and punishing behaviours.

I can see the two broad areas – power and love – as informing human interaction but I am happy with neither the language nor the entailments of such a framework. The term 'power', like it or not, willy-nilly carries with it overtones of coercion, of force, threat and domination. In some circumstances, such considerations may be salient, but in many, what is being transacted is more a matter of who has the right to do something rather than who in the final analysis can make something happen. This is not a quibble – a play on words to evade the point – but a matter of substance. In some societies, dominance and submission may well be the grounds against which social actors perform. This does not appear to me to be the circumstance which currently obtains in the United Kingdom, or in Friction Free Castings. More importantly, the notion of power implies that it is something that is done to you or that you exercise in relation to someone else. It misses entirely the aspect of 'authority' which I take to be important, that is that we each need it and seek it; not to exercise it but to be 'bonded' by it. Authority, unlike power, has implications of care and maintenance. When my parents exercised authority over me, it was (theoretically) for my own good; the exercise of 'power' entails no such thoughts. It is a more naked, self-serving term and is heavily instrumental; although ultimately based upon consent, it has an asymmetry about it which does not appear to accord with the emergent, shared, improvisational nature of social and organizational life as I am attempting to depict it.

Nor does the term 'love' accord well with the kind of interactions with which I am concerned. It is altogether too strong a word, with overtones of surrendering to an emotion, of being out of control. I do not wish to avoid the emotional aspects of referents – indeed, as will be seen, they are central to my argument – but I need a language which has at least a surface validity, one which would not be denied by the social actors it purports to depict. If I am uncomfortable with notions of love and hate being applied to George, Paul and the others (or any other actors in organizations), then you can guarantee they would be completely thrown by it. 'Fraternity' – a state of friendly, brotherly relations – is, as I will demonstrate, a more appropriate term, although its manifestation at times may be little different from that which is entailed in the concept of love.

I prefer the term 'authority' because my experience has been that the exercise of power is not seen to be reasonable in any organization; those who hold power seek to have it legitimized:

> One generally shuns the coercive label like the plague, takes pains to deny that he is bribing others when he is offering them inducements, and represents himself as a persuader – if possible, as someone using 'rational persuasion'.[31]

The most important feature of authority is that it is identified with legitimacy. Max Weber, an influential writer on the subject, held that people will not obey those they think of as illegitimate. For him, and for others, we can always tell when a sense of authority exists in an organization or a society: it is when people *voluntarily* obey their leaders. I will have more to say about this approach to authority in a moment; before doing so, however, I wish to capture the notion of construction involved in Weber's definition. Authority is not a thing; it is a relationship created, sustained and modified by those party to it. It is an image of strength, stability and security; it is continually subject to appraisal and revision. It is the search for solidity and strength in others (or in institutions) which will seem like a thing, but is an act of imagination, a construction, a fiction. In its crudest form, one of the parties, in this example a tyrant, says, 'Here I am, strong and dependable. I will take care of your needs and guide you to the promised land', and the other party, the victim, submits totally. Such behaviour is rarely found in organizations, but, as I will seek to illustrate, there is considerable and continuous improvisation around images of authority in each and every organization. Fraternity – the other fundamental referent – is based upon the need to belong, the notion of 'us' as opposed to 'them' and, occasionally, as opposed to 'me'.

Authority and fraternity connect me to my colleagues but each also binds me to them; I need to participate in authority, I need to be nurtured or to nurture but, if I am to survive as an individual, I fear enslavement. I need to belong, to share with others, but do not wish to be possessed by others.

The need for authority is basic.[32] George is looking for it; Paul is ambivalent about offering it (as many of us are in the latter half of the twentieth century, having been schooled to distrust it) and is probably not surprised to find his offer spurned. It is my contention that many of us wish to be authorities or in authority. This is certainly true of Friction Free Castings and of virtually every other organization with which I have been involved. A great many actions and interactions may be seen as relating to ambivalent feelings around the notion of authority. Each of us seeks to provide or have provided for us guidance, security and stability; simultaneously, many of us doubt our own ability and/or that of other people to provide these goodies. George, relying upon his authority as Finance Director, offers guidance (however ineptly expressed) about how we should regard the latest figures. Paul is not enamoured of this guidance, does not respect George as an authority and offers what he, Paul, takes to be reassurance. The quibble about the interpretation of the figures marks the more fundamental, more emotional struggle about authority; neither party will grant the other it and feelings run high as each tries to assert his position and deny that of the other. There can be no doubting the theme which underpins both Paul's final statement – 'I don't like the stance you are taking, George, I don't like it one little bit.' – and George's response to it – 'Of course not!' Don't mess me about, I'm not a child, I will not take that kind of chastisement, that form of guidance. Both parties are angry at the conclusion of the episode, neither's desire for authority is satisfied; the struggle will continue.

What then is authority? There's the rub; it is easier to apprehend than to comprehend. The image of authority which sticks in my mind comes from working for an all too brief span with a senior executive in a company. Some executives have a presence which is larger than life, they have a kind of star quality which, as it were, hedges them about with an aura of competence; it invites deference. The company had a number of such characters chosen, some of us would declare mockingly, for their height and looks, groomed in the company charm school and set to guide us lesser, spotty mortals. Fred had some of these characteristics, but not all of them; he was tall, was good looking and well spoken, but he did not move with his own follow spotlight, he didn't signal delight in himself as some of the others did ('if he were an ice cream he would eat himself'). He was a relaxed individual and gave the impression of being in complete control. He was apparently totally self-assured and appeared not to need to raise his voice to convince either himself or others. He was certainly not authoritarian, he encouraged ideas and clearly reflected upon them before deciding the most appropriate course of action.

Some executives raise the voice, become involved in contests over authority and direction, cajole, threaten, exhort. Fred did none of this (or, at least, I never experienced it). With him there was no coercion, no threat; simply a senior executive trying to help me sort the problem out, someone who was helping me do my job better. It was not evident then, but is now, that in many cases (by no means all), doing the job better meant doing it Fred's way because he knew and guided me, in a relaxed but nonetheless effective manner, to the correct solution.

It should be clear that I liked Fred, but he also inspired a form of fear in me. I remember being in one particular meeting with him. Earlier I had decided to leave the company for a career as an itinerant academic. He had been 'disappointed', but had understood my decision and had only been concerned that my spell with the company which he had persuaded me to join had not adversely affected my academic pretensions. The later meeting in question, involving several executives, was an important one and, since my mind was elsewhere, I did not perform particularly well; I didn't mess it up totally, but I was not up to standard. At one point, Fred looked across at me and said very quietly and very carefully,

'Perhaps you would take us through this last bit again, Iain, and do a proper job. I am not sure that you convinced too many of us of the necessity of this investment.' I was not living up to my reputation and he was not going to let me or anyone else get away with sloppy work. I made a proper job of it the second time around.

So what are the elements of an authoritative person? Fred was (is) relaxed, controlled, self-assured, experienced and knowledgeable, had superior judgement, had an ability to set standards and cause others to meet them, was undogmatic, had an ability to impose a non-demonstrative discipline. And he had integrity, I sensed that his authority was disinterested, guiding and reassuring me; it was not an expression of domination, I was not being exploited, manipulated or manoeuvred. I was a willing recipient of something that I took to be solid, stable and geared towards my needs and my overall welfare.

By now, some of you may be feeling distinctly uncomfortable; despite my disclaimers, you will have perceived something malign or exploitative in the relationship. You may have ascribed naivety to me and have taken it that my spaniel-like attachment to Fred was a consequence of previously poor relations with my father, inadequate potty training or whatever. On the other hand, you may grant that my upbringing was right and proper save that it did not equip me for the cynical manipulation of an expert in human relations whose primary motive, however well disguised from me, was the pursuit of self-aggrandizement and/or company profit. If you harbour such doubts, or variants of them, fine; you are exhibiting exactly the ambivalence about authority which I take to be characteristic of much of what passes for everyday interaction in organizations. Our present condition is that we fear authority; we anticipate that others and perhaps even ourselves will use whatever brief authority we have to do harm or, at best, simply serve a self-interest.

I recognize no *infallible* authority, even in special questions; consequently, whatever respect I may have for the honesty and sincerity of an individual, I have no absolute faith in any person. Such a faith would be fatal to my reason, to my liberty, and even to the success of my undertakings; it would immediately transform me into a stupid slave, the tool of other people's will and interests.'[33]

The performers at Friction Free Castings were completely knotted up around authority and they felt bad about it. Their inability to break out of the patterns of rejection made authority a central concern for each and every one of them. George struggles with Paul, the group with Paul and George, Eric with Alec and Hugh, all of them with Manchester. What they are looking for in rejecting each other's pretensions is an image of strength, an interpretation of power that gives the unstable consequences of control and influence some legitimacy, however temporary.

The dilemma of our times, as Richard Sennett so clearly expresses it, is that we are often attracted to strong figures we do not believe to be legitimate.[34] What were formerly legitimate images of authority, parents, teachers, owners, managers or whatever, have, in the past hundred years or so, become less legitimate. Nonetheless, the notion of 'the boss' or 'the gaffer' still translates into an image of strength, someone who will 'direct' and show the way; the more assured he or she is, the more moral force he or she appears to exert, the more we are drawn to them whilst, simultaneously, struggling to deny their claims to legitimacy since I, like you, am a free person. What distinguishes much of improvisation around issues of authority is that social actors such as George and the others perform in opposition to that which attracts them. Their behaviour is a counterpoint to the original melody, a descant which is inextricably bound to the theme which gives rise to it. We are attracted to the idea of voluntary obedience and, at the same, repelled or belittled by the thought of it. Alec's ability to persuade and argue are second to none, he attracts others to his position because of his skill and because of it is he is distrusted. In a sense, the group at Friction Free Castings is as much held together by its disaffections, its rejections, as by anything else. The emotions generated by the improvisations, the antagonistic, contrapuntal variations upon authority, define them. The social actors at Friction Free Castings endlessly perform variations on the same theme. They reject each other's claims for authority, but nonetheless stay on stage; they do not get up and leave. George attacks Paul and the rest but paradoxically marks his need for their acceptance in the very act of rejecting them and their claims; they reciprocate. He is bonded to them in displays of rejection.

To be sure, George and the rest may feel they have good reason to reject Paul's authority; he may use it to damage them. It would also be true, however, that they reject him (and each other) because they do not feel any one of them is strong enough. As will be shown later, there were plenty of such comments made within Friction Free Castings: 'What we need is firm leadership.' Part of the knotting up over authority may be that those who claim authority or have it thrust upon them are seen to be not up to it – to be too weak rather than too strong. In either case, too strong or too weak, threatening or impotent, the people we reject help us to define what form of authority we do want. Alec, Derek and some of the others do not want Paul and George agreeing the figures in Manchester, they appear to want authority for the group, but who is 'in' and who is 'out'? Will not the group, in turn, become a potentially destructive force? Such matters constitute the compulsive if inarticulated focusing of attention; without resolution of those issues, little or no technical work can get done. And since authority is always a matter of interpretation, it is always in the process of being resolved.

The other referent for improvisation is what I have termed fraternity.[35] It also is a two-faced concept: each of us both seeks and fears connections to others. We wish to be included but on terms that do not suffocate us. At the same time, in being included we exclude others, sometimes with considerable force and venom. Fraternity, therefore, may be seen as one other emotional bond – it connects and binds and our appreciation of it, our relation to it, is likely to to be a matter of considerable ambivalence and subject to frequent adjustments.

Friction Free Castings, as any other organization, consists of a series of fraternities: alliances or relationships which are important both to those in them and those out. Occasionally the entire group is bonded, as when they attack those 'bloody idiots' at Manchester. Most of the time, however, they show no such unity although they are attracted to the notion of the team or the group. This can be most clearly seen in their interaction around the figures which have been sent to Manchester; it is probably worth repeating this to save you skipping back and forth:

Alec: Hang on a minute, George. There's something wrong with these figures, isn't there?

George: I shouldn't think so.
Alec: Page twenty-three. Column . . . [*counts along*] One, two, three . . . seven. Forecast figures eighty-four/eighty-five. [*There is a scurrying of pages as most search for the relevant passage. Derek is now paying close attention, as are Eric, Hugh and Paul who has rejoined the group.*]
George: Yes. [*A non-statement; cold, uninviting.*]
Derek: What's the problem, Alec?
Alec: Well, my copy says eleven million. Margin of eleven million.
Derek: So does mine. So what? Doesn't it tally or something? Mistake in the adding up?
Alec: [*Ignoring the questions*] How did you arrive at that figure, George?
George: The sum of columns four and six, less the numbers in five.
Alec: I can see that. I don't want the technical answer – I can do that sum for myself. It's the eleven million I'm bothered about. That wasn't the figure we agreed last time.
George: I know.
Alec: [*Consults his papers*] We agreed seventeen million.
George: Yes. [*He begins to shuffle his papers, looks towards Paul. There is a silence; it is clear that he is not going to volunteer anything further.*]
Alec: And that's what went to Manchester some [*consults his papers once more*] six weeks ago.
George: Yes.
Alec: What are these figures then?
George: Revised ones.
Alec: I can see that. Revised by whom?
George: [*Looks towards Paul who continues to avoid eye contact*] By me.
Hugh: What is the status of these figures? Does Manchester have these or the earlier ones?
George: They have these now.

There is an embarrassed silence. George gazes down at his papers. Everyone waits for someone else to break the silence, to say the unsayable.

Alec: But these are not agreed figures.

George: [*Looking towards Paul – again no response*] They are.

Derek: What Alec is really saying, but is too polite to say, is that
            it is up to this group to decide what figures go forward.
            It's our decision and we certainly didn't agree these.

Alec: We must look a right load of idiots up in Manchester;
            from seventeen million down to eleven in six weeks
            including a three week shutdown! A barrow load of
            monkeys could come up with figures like that!

Eric: Got us in one! A load of monkeys.

George: The figures were revised by me and agreed with Paul. I
            had another look at what was being forecast and decided
            what had been sent up was not achievable. In fact, I
            didn't think eleven million was – more like four ...
            [*laughter and head shaking around the table*] Paul would
            not have that, so we sent eleven million in.

Alec: And we are supposed to be committed to that, are we?

Paul: Look, there is no point in getting excited about it. The
            figures don't mean anything; they will change again –
            they always do. We seem to be making a great fuss about
            nothing ...

Derek: About who decides. That's what.

George: Look, it was holiday time – you were all away. Someone
            had to make a decision – Christ, surely we don't have to
            agree everything all of the time? All of us together?

A number of separate conversations break out. The telephone
whistles and Paul crosses to it, turning half towards the wall to
whisper confidentially into it. Derek Morgan rises and heading
towards the toilet says to no one in particular:

Derek: What a way to run a ship!

On the surface this is a matter of figures, but enacted against
both referents: authority and fraternity. Who has the authority to
agree these figures and what is our response as a group to them? In
revealing the lack of commitment to the returns, in commenting
about the decision process – 'About who decides. That's what.' –
Alec, Derek and the rest are indicating what the ideal circumstance

should be. They use a negative to point a positive, relations are revealed to be less than fraternal, but the implication is that they ought to be together on this (and, presumably, a number of other issues).

The downside of the fraternal bond is explicitly stated by George:

George: Look, it was holiday time – you were all away. Someone had to make a decision – Christ, surely we don't have to agree everything all of the time? All of us together?

Even in rejecting this notion, George is offering the importance of fraternity. He may be against it, since it ties him in ways he does not like, but were it not an implicit issue, he would have nothing to oppose and the behaviour would not occur.

Fraternity is a referent to the scene which occurs between Eric, Hugh and Alec. The subcommittee has excluded Eric from its deliberations and is now seeking to 'push things through'. Again this is a matter of authority as well as fraternity, but both Hugh and Alec act in concert to deflect Eric's questions and they collude in a classic piece of pairing:

Alec: [*whispering loudly to Hugh*] I don't know why we bother to spend so much time deciding things, some clown always knows better.

Shortly these same two directors are to object fiercely to being excluded from the process of sending the forecast to Manchester. Social actors move in and out of bonds of fraternity and are likely to experience considerable emotion as a consequence: at one and nearly the same time they both need and reject each other. We are interdependent, but are urged to be independent. The managers in Friction Free Castings are expected to cooperate (and expect to cooperate) but are assessed and assess themselves in terms of their ability to stand aside from their colleagues. A good manager coordinates the work of others, he directs and guides others, is not seduced by them; he or she is independent, self-possessed, more influencing than reactive. Self-possessed, not possessed by others appears to be a key attribute and yet, at another level, we 'know' that we need others to achieve ends impossible to achieve alone. The dilemma is that in seeking autonomy and stressing self-reliance we are unable to achieve our ends, but in bonding with others we lose our independence.

Some pages back I made the bold assertion that there was nothing else to observe in these or any other kinds of interaction but technical activities and improvisation around issues of authority and fraternity. I now wish to make another such assertion to the effect that a great deal of that which is expressed as emotion arises from improvisation around these two referents. Bonds are emotional ties, they are matters of consequence, and as they fluctuate so do our feelings. I choose the term 'bond' since it expresses at one and the same time a sense of uniting and constraining; it also conveys an emotional rather than a simply legal, contractual relationship.[36] As will be seen, I am particularly anxious to highlight this aspect of my definition since I hold (in common with but a few others) that individuals, groups, organizations, institutions are emotionally rather than cognitively bonded.[37] Authority and fraternity connect me to my colleagues but each also binds me to them. I need to belong, but do not wish to be possessed by others or, at the other extreme, be totally rejected by them. Indeed, I will go further and propose that bonds of authority and fraternity unite and divide each and every organization and that the emotion which suffuses improvisations around these referents is the medium through which actions are held together or separated. These assertions are sufficiently novel (though by no means original) and are of such consequence to my overall view of behaviour in organizations that they are worth spending a page or two in expanding.

It will be recalled that in outlining what I took to be the Goffmanesque, strategic interaction perspective, I pointed to a number of difficulties. Pre-eminent amongst these was the observation that there is little evidence to suggest that the usual stance of any of us as social actors is one in which we calculate possible returns before we act; on the contrary – as I have tried to show above – most people most of the time improvise behaviour with little or no conscious reflection. Most courses of action are taken for granted. Despite my blow-by-blow description of the interaction of the executives at Friction Free Castings, it must not be taken as a depiction of their experience at a cognitive level. To be sure, those concerned do pay attention to the content of what is being said, but adjust to each other emotionally at a non-conscious level as issues of authority and fraternity become salient.

Stretching these ideas a little, it is possible to claim that the entire organization of Friction Free Castings for much of the time consists of a series of scripts which broadly uphold improvisations around these twin referents. Just as I have attempted to show that this particular group upholds a routine which celebrates where the members stand *vis-à-vis* each other on these dimensions, so one could outline relations throughout the organization in these terms. Friction Free Castings is the sum of repetitive behaviours which occur between social actors around matters of authority and fraternity. To George, Paul, Alec and the others, what they do and how they feel appears natural and appropriate. No matter what you and I may think of it, no matter what happens elsewhere in their organization, the pattern of improvisation which recurs virtually every time they sit around this particular table in this particular grouping is something which holds them together and apart and defines them as an entity.

Collins[38] refers to the emotions which surround such improvisation as the 'glue' bonding social structures together and one cannot but agree with him. He does not take his analysis far enough, but nevertheless captures neatly what I have been rattling on about in these few pages in his assertion that: 'People follow routines because they feel natural or appropriate ... The underlying emotional dynamics ... centers on feelings of membership in coalitions.' And, I would add, on aspects of authority.

It is, of course, odd to talk of emotions constituting the 'glue' of organizations when the kinds of performances depicted in these pages are addressed. It is odd but, for all its apparent contradiction, valid. The point is that organizations are not cognitively bonded; for the most part, social actors do not reflect, plan, select alternatives, act and then evaluate their actions. They simply perform, that is to say they bring to fruition scripts which are of long standing and are no longer conscious ways of behaving. Associated with the scripts are a range of emotions which are triggered by cues which themselves are barely perceptible to consciousness. It is these repeated performances and their accompanying emotions (which are in fact an intrinsic part of the performance) which form the pattern of the organization as a whole. It does not matter that the performers display antagonisms and antipathies; organizations, paradoxically, may be held together by disaffections as much as by agreements. What is important is that the patterns, however apparently dysfunctional, are repeated; should the pattern be broken, the organization is no longer what it was. Imagine, if you will, a rewrite of the discussion between Paul and George along the following lines:

George: . . . so for the third year running we are turning in a loss.
Paul: . . . three years in a row. I know we have looked at this every month and it is no surprise to any of us, but is there something we have missed, George, something that we ought to have done and have not? We have got the productivity figures up, sales seem to be up . . .
George: True. Some of the trends are in the right direction but we still have not cracked it. Alec and I were talking about this the other day and he seemed to think it was more a matter of what the competitors are up to than anything else . . .
   [*Looks to Alec*]
Alec: Yes, well . . .

I do not need to go on. It is fantasy, after all, if not fairy tale; we only need a kiss from Hugh to turn Eric into a prince and it will become totally ridiculous. It should be clear, however, that the emotional tone of such a conversation, were it to be enacted without tongues in cheek, would be very different to that which normally obtains between these actors. I have chosen my words carefully. Improvisation occurs primarily at an emotional level; each of us apprehends what is going on and performs in line with the emotional implications of that which we pick up *without* reflection. This is not to deny that we can reject and inhibit an action, but simply to state that in many circumstances we do not. We simply perform. The structure of the organization is the repeated actions, the emotional bondedness, not simply the content of what is said.

This has been a long exposition and it is time to pull it together; in the next chapter I will have more to say about improvisation, about authority and fraternity and about emotion; for the moment, I will close with a brief reprise of the main themes, utilizing whenever appropriate terms drawn from the theatre.[39]

The first theme was that of pragmatism, the essence of which I took to be the notion of ourselves as products of and producers of the society in which we find ourselves. Following the ideas of Peirce (as expressed by Collins), I took it that each one of us is the sum total of our thoughts and, in turn, that this sum is always a 'historical bundle of [our] society's experience'. Given the potential social nature of our minds, it seemed logical to pick up the ideas of the interactionists, notably Mead and Blumer, and see how we incorporate the ideas of society into our everyday interaction. Mead, like Peirce, recognized the importance of symbols and provides us with a reasonable, coherent account of the development of our abilities to interact with others. Utilizing notions derived from subsequent generations of writers, I attempted to flesh this account out by introducing terms such as presentation of self, altercasting, the negotiating of order and the like; all pretty standard stuff, but essential to the development of the next stage of my argument.

Here, whilst not denying the possibility of strategic interaction (the conscious awareness of what is occurring and the conscious manipulation of behaviour), I asserted that much of social and organizational life was not strategic, it was (and is) a matter of scripts and performance. Scripts are routine, predictable sequences in which the performers run off action (without reflection). They are, however, rarely tightly scripted in the sense that each line is specified and every gesture is controlled. Scripts in organizations are of a much looser construction; we know in general terms what is expected of us and what to expect of others, and we improvise in line with these expectations.

Underlying our improvisations, however, are a couple of basic themes or referents. All performances at executive level are concerned with technical matters (budgeting, planning, monitoring and the like) and with matters of authority and fraternity. These twin themes constitute the basis for all interaction and are the source of a great deal of emotion. Both generate considerable ambivalence; we both desire and reject authority and fraternity, although only in rare cases do we explicitly address either theme.

It is well over a hundred years since Charles Sanders Peirce set pen to paper and we have come a long way since that time in understanding how we interact. Many of his ideas have not stood the test of time but one aspect of his work resonates still: the insight that 'mental processes are operating unconsciously as long as the habits of connection are firmly established and nothing happens to disturb the smooth flow of inference'.[40] Scripts are the epitome of such processes and they are enacted with emotion in every organization each and every day. The implications of this statement will be explored in the next chapter.

3 Theme and Variations

This chapter consists largely of a series of scenes or vignettes drawn from executive groups which have been selected to illustrate and develop some of the points made in chapter 2. I will begin with circumstances in which fraternity appears to be the major referent for improvised behaviour. Fraternity, as I have indicated, is a matter of belonging or not belonging to a group, so I will provide examples where aspects of belonging are the issue: matters of individuality, involvement, and trust. I will follow this by illustrations of situations in which authority is the referent, again refining this with examples of dependent disobedience, autonomy and creativity. This categorization is essentially crude and I make no claims that it is exhaustive. It is, of course, also somewhat artificial, since the categories overlap; it should, therefore, be taken as a matter of placing a particular emphasis for heuristic purposes rather than a conclusive indication of observably different states.[1]

In each case I will attempt to place the sequence in context, not only to provide the essential background, but also to highlight the fact that what the actors bring to the group is coloured by the larger organization and their part in it. Placing the scenes in context, of course, also enables me to point out that whatever occurs within the scene has consequences elsewhere. Behaviour is exported as well as imported; what senior members do as members of an executive group impacts upon the organization. It affects the sense of purpose of everyone in the enterprise, energizing them or creating a sense of vulnerability and anxiety.

I begin with scenes drawn to illustrate aspects of fraternity, not because I accord it more importance than authority but because without members there can be no group. I will present and comment upon four scenes in each of which members, or potential members, of particular executive groups struggle with particular aspects of their ambivalence about fraternity. I wish to emphasize that simply bringing executives together into a room at a specified time for some express purpose will not necessarily result in a *group* endeavour. Indeed, the technical or content matter of the meeting may not be resolved because at a conscious or more likely unconscious level, those present are unable or unwilling to deal with 'belonging' in such a session. Dealing with belonging involves matters of individuality, involvement and trust. The first scene highlights aspects of individuality.[2]

Six men are sitting in a large room. It is a converted tithe barn with timbered beams and white stucco walls. The conversion has evidently been undertaken with taste and considerable sums of money have been expended. The barn now serves as a Boardroom with a splendid, highly polished, craftsman-built, rectangular teak table dominating the scene. Around it are arranged some thirty chairs; those to one end are unoccupied and drawn up to the table in disciplined lines, whereas at the other end of the room the chairs are in disarray as their occupants sprawl around the focal position at the head of the table, that of the Managing Director. The room has five large windows providing glimpses of the courtyard beyond, which is backlit with a cold wash of winter sunshine. Heavy velvet curtains floor to ceiling are complemented by expensive carpeting. Portraits of the founding members of the company, evidently dour and no-nonsense men, cover the wall opposite the windows, each a silent witness of the proceedings undertaken in their joint family names.

Philip, who is the Managing Director of one of the subsidiary divisions, is talking. He is a tall, somewhat spare individual with the severe expression one might associate with those whose purpose in life in former times would have been to smell out witchcraft. He has a lean and hungry look, an almost cadaverous appearance exacerbated by his severe, charcoal grey suit, his white shirt and dark blue tie, his cold, rimless spectacles and his sparse grey hair, which he wears cut almost brutally short. He is outlining his intention to undercut his colleagues in a sector of the market hitherto not exploited by his division. His tone throughout is peremptory:

Philip: . . . So, as I see it, that's it. We are going all out for that
            end of the market. We recognize that in so doing we may
            be treading on a few toes, but that's the price that will
            have to be paid.

He places his pen carefully on the table and sits back. The
atmosphere is tense although, at this stage, no one seems prepared
to respond. Eventually Derek, the Managing Director of the parent
company, speaks. A small, somewhat diffident man, he derives his
authority from being a member of the founding family. His face is
destined to join those of his ancestors on the wall. He is dressed
somewhat casually, even unconventionally, in a worn sports jacket
with leather patches at the elbows and cuffs, and tan corduroy
trousers. His ill-fitting shirt is of a loud check and he sports a
bright red tie. He is a good ten years younger than most of his
colleagues – in his early thirties – and is conscious of both his age
and the source of his authority.

Derek: OK. Fine. Thank you, Philip. Very . . . er . . . clear.
            [*Waits. Looks at each person in turn. No one, other than
            Barry, Head of the Service Division, meets his eye.*] Well?
            What do we think? [*No response*] Philip has laid it on the
            line . . . Proposed a course of action . . . which will throw
            us into direct competition with each other . . . What do
            we think? . . . Tony? . . . Michael? . . . Barry?

Barry needs no second invitation. He is a large, florid and
excitable man whose every gesture exudes energy barely under
control. He wears a dark grey suit complete with waistcoat and
sports a bright handkerchief thrust into his top pocket; although
clearly designed for a man of his height and girth, his clothes give
the impression of being about to burst. His hair is unruly, as are his
tie and the papers scattered on the table in front of him. He peers
at his colleagues over the top of his reading glasses which from
time to time he thrusts back upon his nose with clumsy irritation.

Barry: I'm willing to jump in if no one else is. As I see it, what
            Philip is proposing is a direct challenge to the way we
            have operated up till now . . . to be precise and pedantic,

a direct challenge to both Tony and Michael – as Service Division, we follow rather than lead [*derisive laughter around the table*] . . . which won't stop me jumping in. Not to put too fine a point on it, what is being proposed will wreck the company . . . let's not kid ourselves about that . . . It's a complete bollocks for us to set out to screw each other in this fashion . . . .

Philip: Bollocks or not, it's what my division intends to do.

Barry: Not if we don't agree it you're not! That's why we are here – to sort out this kind of thing. You can't just declare you are going to do something like this and expect us to cheer you on, you know.

Philip: I have profit responsibility for my division and am free to determine my markets and my prices.

Barry: Your freedom stops, old son, where my nose begins – to paraphrase somebody or other. It's not up to you – or any one of us – to decide on a shift like that . . .

Tony: He's right, Philip. It's not a runner. It's never been the policy to clash head on in the field.

Neat, precise, the mind of an accountant, the appearance of a business graduate. Thirty-two years old and a rising star in the organization, well organized, smooth, ambitious and cold. Tall, well shaven, neat well trimmed hair, tailored-fit monogrammed shirt, jacket carefully arranged on an adjacent chair. Calculator and a small portable computer on the table before him. Managing Director of one of the other divisions.

Philip: Look, I'm responsible . . . I'm held accountable . . . for the profit, you are as well . . . in pursuit of targets . . .

Barry: [*Interrupting*] Agreed here.

Philip: Put up by me and rubber stamped here . . . in pursuit of them it is up to me how I go about it . . .

Michael: [*Incredulous*] Rubber stamped . . .

Philip: Don't play the innocent, Michael. You know as well as I do . . . you'd be the first to complain if we chucked your figures out.

Barry: [*Cutting across the exchange, ignoring it*] What happens if I decide not to provide the support? Advertising, for example, that's a central service. What if I decide that there is no sense in running campaigns to fight each other?

Philip: It's your job to provide the service, and in any case, we wouldn't be so stupid as to knock each other . . .

Barry: It's my job as a director of the company to maximize overall profit. That's your job as well.

Philip: What I propose will do just that!

Tony: What you propose will lead to anarchy. Simply sticking a load of figures before us and saying 'Take it or leave it' is not the way to go about things . . .

Philip: That's good, coming from you, Tony! What about the decision to go into own brands? As I recall that, you did that without any consultation with us – I knew nothing of it until the goods were on the lorries.

Tony: That was months ago, and in any event, you didn't need to know about it. It didn't affect your division.

Philip: It had implications for the company as a whole – profit implications, policy switches . . .

Tony: Barry knew about it, Derek knew about it . . .

Philip: Derek is behind this proposal of mine. We've discussed it and he's for it. [*This revelation is greeted with surprise by Tony, Michael and Barry.*]

Derek: Yes. I said that I would support it. [*Shuffling and muttering around the table. Philip is clearly pleased with the turn of events. Tony and Michael appear nonplussed. Silence. Barry appears to be weighing up the pros and cons of a course of action. He decides.*]

Barry: So what? So Philip nobbled Derek before the meeting. How does that change anything? He didn't nobble me, or Tony or Michael. As I understand it, in this brave new world we now inhabit, it's not up to Philip and Derek, or Tony and Derek, or, for that matter, *me* and Derek to fix on a one-to-one basis . . . It's up to us. Us as a group. [*There is a long pause. All seem at a loss as to how to proceed.*]

Clearly I do not need to labour the point: Philip epitomizes individuality, just as Barry stands for the power of the group. This kind of conflict is not unusual (it does, of course, also reflect a struggle over authority). Philip's repeated use of the personal pronoun, 'I'm responsible, I'm held accountable' signals his position: the group is there for no other purpose than to 'rubber stamp' his actions. Given his peremptory tone and his dismissive attitude towards his fellow directors, it would be easy to cast Philip as the villain of the piece and to declare that no group can function with someone like this sitting in on it. To make such an assertion (widely shared though it may be) would be profoundly wrong.

The existence of an effective group depends upon connections being made between its members; without links, communications, there is nothing to belong to; nothing but a hollow centre. No successful group *at an executive level* can be founded simply on similarities. The function of the executive is to reconcile differences; for this to occur, these differences, these individualities, must be expressed. But, and here's the rub, the very expression of these individualities appears to threaten the group: 'What you propose will lead to anarchy' in the company and in this group, here and now. Thus the tension and the struggle. What this group does not yet realize and what few groups ever realize is that the tension, although life threatening, is essential to the proper functioning of the group. A successful enterprise is characterized by a senior team in which issues of individuality are frequently encountered. It is not one, however, in which individuality is seen to threaten group solidarity. Quite the reverse; group solidarity is enhanced as members learn to accept and encourage individuality and individuality, in turn, is enhanced as the primacy of the group is affirmed.[3]

An effective executive process is characterized by both individuality and group solidarity; in such a circumstance, the Philips of the world would enjoy freedom of expression, the right to challenge and disagree and be encouraged in these attributes by the Barrys and the Tonys. Unlike the circumstance in which he currently finds himself, Philip would not regard himself as one against the rest needing to enlist the support of the managing director, Derek, to secure his own way. In an effective executive, he would acknowledge the need for a collective goal, the need to subsume some of his views, the need for compromise. The group can only exist and develop *if* individuality is encouraged *and* sufficient connections can be developed to make it worthwhile for individuals to reconcile their differences. A moment's thought will convince even the most sceptical of you that if I do not know where you stand and you do not know my position, our chances of identifying similarities and thus creating a group are slight. Another moment's thought will reveal, however, that our declaration of individuality may well jeopardize any hope of coming together. Thus individuality and conformity are frequent aspects of improvisation in groups. Individuality is clearly related to involvement, to which I now turn.

We have met Alec before, so I do not need to describe him again, but I do need to set the scene because I am about to show him in a novel circumstance. This is Alec and his colleagues *after* both he and they have undergone several sessions looking at themselves and their organization. This is an early meeting of an executive group of a reorganized Friction Free Castings. Eric and Tony have been excluded from the executive meetings; a new man, Tom, has been recruited to head up marketing for the entire organization; and Alec, relieved of his responsibility for production, is now responsible for strategic planning. The executive, still chaired by Paul, is now expressly to be concerned with matters of strategy. Although some work has been done on the role of the meeting and the members, there remains a considerable degree of uncertainty and anxiety as to what, if anything, this revised grouping can achieve together. Alec is pressing for clear statements of policy from his colleagues.[4]

Alec: . . . it seems the best way forward. If we schedule one every week, we can go through it, agree it, revise it or whatever, promulgate it and move on.
George: Beginning with?
Alec: What?
Derek: 'Beginning with.' Who is going to kick off? Whose head is to be first on the block? [*Nervous laughter around the table.*]
Alec: How about yours?
Derek: You can forget that. How about Products? Hugh should be a long way down the line with that now. We have been raking over that ground for months now.
          [*Hugh does not respond*]

Of course, we could ask Tom or Terry – they are the new boys. How about marketing or manufacturing? We need a statement about what they are up to, don't we?

Tom: I am sure we do but I am in no position to give it at the moment. Give me three months and I might be.

Derek: I wasn't serious, Tom, just pulling your leg.

Alec: Someone has to kick off.

George: How about you? You have management services. How about a plan for them we can all look at? You want these policies, you write one.

Alec: Hang on, hang on a minute. *I* don't want these policies. *We* want them.

Paul: Alec's right. They are for us, not him.

George: OK. Accept that. You give *us* your plan, then. Let's stop pissing about and get on with it.

Derek: Who's pissing about, George?

George: You are! If we go along with Alec, and I do, let's get on with it. Shilly-shallying around! Christ, someone has to put up their plan first. Alec suggests it and then will not deliver . . .

Alec: How about you, George . . . .?

George: I haven't got a bloody plan. How do I have one? I service all the rest of you.

Hugh: No reason why you should not lay out some financial policy or strategy.

George: It's been done – it was an integral part of the overall strategy.

Hugh: So was product development, so was personnel and management services . . .

Alec: There doesn't seem to be much point in continuing this, no one wishes to do what I thought we had agreed to do, so we ought to move on to something else. Something we actually intend to do.

Paul: Sounds like you are taking your bat home, Alec.

Alec: Well. Yes I am. We are no further forward after half an hour on this topic. I don't want to push it further . . .

The existence of a group requires connections among its members but, as can be seen from this sequence, these connections cannot be made unless members throw in their lot with others. Throwing in one's lot with others, however, is a potentially risky business. This is evident from Derek's comment, 'Whose head is to be first on the block?' At the manifest, content level of the interaction, fears are being expressed and are picked up in the nervous laughter. At the covert level, potential members pick up what happens when they do participate: they are accused of 'pissing about'. An emergent group norm appears to be that refusing to go along with something, refusing to be the first to offer a policy will be punished. It is to be regarded as inappropriate behaviour. Such an implicit rule, if allowed to develop, will do little to encourage individuals to participate. Virtually everyone in the room, some more than others, is holding back his energies until he knows what the group will be like. It is, however, this very tentativeness that contributes to making the group unsafe. The less Paul, Hugh, Tom and Terry say, the greater the uncertainty about what this situation may demand of any individual and the more difficult it is to establish any connections. Alec, Derek and George pitch in but, in so doing, realize that whatever is happening is not to their liking. Alec clearly and unequivocally withdraws his support from the debate on which policy is to be first on the agenda – he takes his bat home. At the content level, his action signals 'I do not like this interaction, I am getting nowhere, I am better off out of it, someone else can lead the discussions.' Although the discussion has gone on half an hour, it is an early indication of his views about participating in the group. Rather than supporting his view of himself as an effective manager, it is undercutting it and he clearly feels better off out of it. He sees no point in a struggle of himself against the group.

Improvisations around involvement often take the form of accusing others of not participating in the discussions or accusing them, as in this case, of not being willing to *do* something. The dilemma for the group, though not one that is readily understood or articulated, is that for it to be effective members must be given space to *do* things and to reflect upon them, to participate in discussions and to observe them. The notion that he or she that is silent is to be attacked should be resisted, but rarely is. Separating out the volunteers from the non-volunteers, the doers from the observers, the risk takers from the non-risk takers, produces the kind of oscillation that is observable in this instance. Rather than having to respond to the baitings of his colleagues, Hugh should allow his reflection full rein; he should be given space to think about what is occurring and then encouraged to participate in a considered manner. The stigmatizing of those who are not actively pursuing a particular theme is not helpful. On the other hand, unless someone says something, takes some action, there is nothing to observe and reflect upon (except, of course, the absence of action); so participation is also necessary, but if it receives the kind of treatment evident here, there is little enough reason for anyone to persist.

This brings me to my next scene: this time the emphasis is upon trust.[5] Before we are willing to trust others, we want to know how they will respond to us, but, as with involvement, in order to discover how others will respond, someone must be willing to risk something. 'Hello, how are you?' may signal a degree of involvement but it has nothing much to do with trust. In this extract Hugh is revealing that he does not agree with something which, for the past fourteen months, he has appeared to go along with; he is taking a considerable risk:

Hugh: I am not sure that I agree with that.
Alec: What?
Hugh: The need for an explicit document setting out target dates for new product development.
Alec: But that's the basis of our entire strategy.
George: It's what we agreed to months ago. You and Alec spent days putting it all together. Every customer, every product, line by line . . .
Paul: Just a minute, George – let's hear what Hugh is saying before we start in on him.
George: I'm not getting at him . . . I just want to understand what we have all been doing these past few months.
Alec: What are you saying, Hugh? That we have all been wasting our time because you didn't really go along with what you agreed?
Derek: That explains why we never seem to have proper product review meetings.
Paul: Hang on. Hang on. Hugh . . . [*invites him by gesture to contribute*]

Hugh: Well, it's just that I have reservations, that's all. Can't subscribe to this notion of everything being planned ... customers don't work that way. Product development isn't like that – you spend time with your key customers and gradually something emerges. We are behind on all the dates specified.

George: By you! By you!

Hugh: By us, George, by us and, yes, I had a hand in it. I went along with it but I am telling you now I do not believe that is the way to go about it ... It doesn't happen like that. You cannot deliver new products to order. Look at the money we have been throwing at the 230, and what can we show for it? Nothing, or virtually nothing. To be sure, there could be a market for it if we had it but we don't, and meanwhile we neglect the areas that we have established products in ...

[*He tails off. There is a long silence, eventually broken by Alec in a tone of quiet accusation.*]

Alec: But you went along with this, Hugh. You were responsible for implementing the strategy. A strategy you disagreed with.

Hugh: That's correct. But you have to remember where we started from ... We were in no position to agree anything, we had nothing going for us a year or so ago. Something agreed, even this, was better than nothing.

George: But it's fundamental. If you did not agree at the time you should have said so.

Hugh: I did on several occasions. Probably not strongly enough ... then I went along with it. And ever since then, we have all avoided talking about our lack of progress – me included.

Paul: Until today.

Hugh: Until today.

This is anything but a trivial exchange. Hugh, for whatever reason, has decided to declare where he stands; in so doing, he is risking rejection by his colleagues. Their initial reactions are such as to confirm his fears, only Paul's persistent intent to give Hugh space to declare himself prevents an instant kangaroo court. The ambivalence is evident here in the desire of some members, notably Paul, to hear the 'bad news', as it were, and the desire of others to shut it out, to react sharply to it and close down the conversation. Hugh, however, in describing his real position on product development, not only brings out into the open concern over that particular aspect of policy, but also invites the group to consider the way it is behaving as a group. At one level he is focusing upon content, at another the process; consciously or unconsciously he is offering feedback about the group. It does not work well if it takes fourteen months for someone to own his disagreement.

Lacking this kind of disclosure, the group cannot and will not learn. Negative feedback tells the members that it is not working well and, *if handled well*, allows some reflection to occur as to why it is not working, what alternatives are open to it with what consequences. Interestingly enough, for Hugh to offer this kind of feedback – 'we have all avoided talking about our lack of progress' – he must minimally trust the group. That trust, of course, will rapidly be reassessed if he receives severe punishment for his revelations. From the perspective of the other members of the executive group, it may look very different. Hugh may be seen as a person of little standing in the group because he does not often contribute and when he does it is usually to make a 'negative comment'. If this is so, then the present comments will not be well received. The lack of progress will not be the group's responsibility but Hugh's; we (members of the group) gave him every opportunity to speak up but he never did. Thus an important learning opportunity may be lost. Closely related to this response is the difficulty that any group has in hearing negatives. Negative feedback, indication of when things are not working, is essential to the proper functioning of a group, but frequently the message does not get through the noise. Members may experience considerable anxiety about the manner in which their competence as a group is questioned and, as a direct consequence, spend time and energy handling this collective emotional disturbance rather than addressing the problem. It is very common for groups to turn upon members who give negative feedback to them.[6] This group, you will not be surprised to know, was no exception and gave Hugh a hard time, accusing him of all manner of things whilst simultaneously asserting that if it were really a matter of their behaviour, they would be only too willing to correct it.

The ambivalence which characterizes so many of these kinds of improvisations is obvious. If the group is to be effective, it needs the kind of discouraging information that people like Hugh offer, but to offer such material individuals must feel that they can trust their colleagues to deal with it and with them as providers of it. The group cannot develop without the material, but without development, without a kind of group maturity, individuals risk rejection if they offer criticism. And – you have guessed it – without negative as well as positive feedback, the group cannot reach maturity. So once again we have similar dynamics: an attraction to providing information that will build trust, but a movement away from so doing because the group is not trustworthy.

So much for fraternity as a referent for improvisation; more, much more, could be written about it and the categories could, no doubt, be further subdivided or addressed in a different fashion.[7] I turn now to the other referent: authority. I will begin with some general comments upon authority, picking up from where I left off in the previous chapter, and will then provide some scenes reflecting dependent disobedience, autonomy and creativity.

Usually authority is thought of as something that flows down from above: a boss (such as Paul) derives his or her authority from those higher up and subordinates accept their subordination as part of the terms and conditions under which they work. As I pointed out earlier, however, authority is not a thing; it is created between individuals, sustained and changed by those same individuals. It is better to talk of a process of authorizing rather than a matter of authority. Notwithstanding Paul's formal title and the powers invested in him by those beyond him in Manchester, Paul's authority ultimately derives from the willingness of his colleagues at Friction Free Castings to accept his direction. In a sense, they authorize him to enact certain things on their behalf.[8] Whatever he does as a member of their particular executive team is dependent as much upon his claim as of right to do it as upon the members' willingness to give over part of their rights to him. He has no authority – no *voluntary* followership – without them and they have no leadership without him (or someone else) assuming it.

The ambivalence manifests itself around the desire to be led and the equally strong desire in groups of this kind for individuals to be treated as equals. If Paul has the authority, if the rest of the team authorizes him to act on their behalf, to direct and lead them, this appears to imply that none of them has authority. As a direct consequence, all concerned may become confused about authority and successfully deny it to any one person or group. Paul, in this particular instance, does not behave in an authoritative fashion probably because his colleagues (and technical subordinates) will not allow him to do so, but also because he appears to believe that acting in such a manner (were it to be sanctioned) would imply that no one else had authorization to do anything. The result is, of course, predictable: everyone is frustrated and irritated. No one feels authorized to do anything (remember the discussion about the Manchester figures) and demands for action increase. Given this level of ambivalence, nothing can be done, and the feeling of frustration becomes stronger; but so does the fear of any one person taking over and making others 'do something'. The resistance to authorize anyone to lead the group out of the problem that the lack of authority has created becomes greater and greater the more the need for strong leadership increases. If in such a circumstance a group were to authorize a leader to take 'firm action', it would apparently involve every member giving up his or her rights to take back the authority; the leader may take the group firmly in the direction that some, many or all of them do not wish to go, yet they authorized it. On occasions, members of groups desperately seek to authorize someone, anyone, to lead them out of the wood whilst simultaneously denying this person the support necessary to a leader.

The extract which follows is an example of what may be termed dependent disobedience – a circumstance in which bonds of rejection are evident, in which one individual depends upon the person with the more power, but signals his/her hostility whilst submitting. The extract with which I began this book, the interaction between Paul and George, is a good example of the kind of thing I am seeking to articulate, as is this scene from the interaction of a number of executives responsible for the manufacturing and sales of a luxury motor car.[9]

Seven men are seated around a round table in the Chief Executive's office. The table is glass topped and is of a strikingly modern design, as are the chairs and the rest of the furniture in the room. It appears to be of Italian origin and contrasts sharply with the essentially traditional character of the product and the company. The Chief Executive is in his mid forties, young for the industry, is dressed in a lightweight suit, plain linen shirt and an aggressively bright, striped tie. He has been with the company less than a year and has a background and impressive record in marketing. He is not an engineer. The others in the room, with the exception of the finance director, are engineers and hitherto all chief executives have been engineers.

The Chief Engineer is speaking as we join the group. He is a thickset individual with a shock of greying hair sticking up as though attracted by a magnet above him. He is regarded by his colleagues as 'solid', a term of approbation in this company where 'fly-by-nights' are despised. A 'solid' person like Frank has 'nous', has 'been around', is considered 'to know the industry' and has 'done it'. By comparison, characters such as David, the Chief Executive – 'something of a fly-by-night' – lack these qualities. Peering over his half glasses, Frank is probably well aware that David has been brought in to 'ginger things up', and he is certainly aware that a number of his friends have recently been dismissed. The discussion is focusing upon the inability of the company to plan and meet launch dates for new models. Frank is seeking to attribute blame well away from the Engineering departments:

Frank: It's on and off in this place, at least it has been for the past few years, go and no go. Never know where we are.

David: I am not talking about the past, Frank, I am talking about now.

Frank: Can't understand now without talking about the past, David. Most of us have been around a long time; we've seen it all before: ra ra ra one minute, hang on, whoa, back up a bit the next. That's no climate to plan and deliver in.

David: Why are we late on the T90 now? Today. This morning?

Frank: In what sense late? We are not . . .

David: Come on, come on, Frank, you know what I am talking about. By your own figures we are at least fourteen months behind the schedule your boys provided a couple of years ago.

Frank: Engineering is not like soap flakes, you know, David. It takes time, there are problems, *engineering* problems to overcome. Not a matter of packaging, substantial problems, we can't just come up with any old solution.

David: OK. So why put out a schedule you don't intend to meet?

Frank: We did intend to meet it, at the time it seemed reasonable, it's just that you can't foresee every problem.

David: But you've never met a schedule, have you? You have been in charge since 1973 and no car has been launched on the scheduled date. Eleven years, four new models, all late. All engineering problems, were they?

Frank: Right . . .

David: Wrong! All scheduling problems. Let's be honest, Frank, the planning and scheduling is up the spout *and* the development side is happy just to noodle along. It's got to change, we can't afford to be missing the market time after time.

Frank: Are you telling me to put more pressure on my lads? They are working themselves silly as it is . . .

David: I am, Frank, I am; more pressure, more productivity. Let's get it right.

Frank: Well, we'd better have that minuted, hadn't we? When the cars start coming back, we'd better know where the pressure to cut corners came from, hadn't we? I am telling you as an engineer that whatever time it takes, it takes, and there's nothing you or I can do about that – things either work or they do not.

David: It's gold plated, Frank, it's belt and braces; everything over-engineered, overdone. I want the cars out faster, on the roads, money in the bank.

Frank: Are you telling me to cut corners?

David: I am asking you to put in realistic schedules, engineer sensible cars and meet the target dates.

Frank: If that's what you want, I'll pass it on. I can tell you, though, it will not be appreciated. It's not the way we make cars.

I could go on (it was an interesting meeting) but my intent is not to give a complete account of what makes these particular people tick, but rather to illustrate what I, following closely the ideas of Richard Sennett, take to be dependent disobedience.[10] The very act of disobeying, with all its anxieties and ramifications, actually knits these characters together. It is important to note that Frank is not rebelling *against* David, he is not saying your authority counts for nothing, so forget it. He is saying, tell me what you want and then I will at one and the same time signal both my acceptance of it and my hostility towards it. It is rebellion within authority. Frank's words are symbols of transgression rather than acts of revolt. Someone rebelling against authority would directly challenge David, would assert his own independence and would challenge the Chief Executive to do something about it. Frank does not do this. His hostility is, initially, covert: 'There are . . . *engineering* problems to overcome. Not a matter of packaging.' When pressed it becomes overt: 'I am telling you as an engineer that whatever time it takes, it takes, and there's nothing you or I can do about that – things either work or they do not.' Direct enough, you may think, but not so. Frank does not say, trust me to do the job or sack me. He does not openly rebel, however close he may appear to come to it; indeed, he shows his dependent disobedience by demanding to be told what to do: 'Are you telling me to cut corners?', and is satisfied, concluding in splendid fashion: 'If that's what you want, I'll pass it on. I can tell you, though, it will not be appreciated. It's not the way we make cars.'

The central character for Frank in this interchange is, of course, David. He is in thrall to him – bonded to him by the very act of disobedience. Frank is not independent, or yet autonomous. He does not stand alone, he needs a David to oppose; he disobeys him, opposes him but David regulates the terms, he controls the script. In effect, Frank is asking, 'Are you strong enough to take me on? The answer is clearly yes, so I will do what you say but I will not own my dependence upon you, I will specifically deny it, even though in the act of so doing I actually demonstrate it.'

My next extract illustrates autonomy and will serve as a contrast with this last extract.[11] Rather than warn you what to look out for, I invite you to review the material yourself before I offer an interpretation. The setting is a conference room within the

production or creative side of a television company. The meeting
has been called by the Managing Director of the company to
discuss 'programming matters' and is attended by senior members
of staff concerned with operations (the technical, scheduling and
engineering staff) and those concerned with the making of
programmes (the head of drama, light entertainment, news,
outside broadcasts and features). Neville, the Managing Director,
has been with the company two years and has a background in
journalism and publishing; to Tony Dancer, Director of Programmes and a director of the company, man and boy in the television
industry, Neville is not 'one of us'. Neville, himself, regards his
lack of television experience as an asset; he is young, pleased with
his abilities and achievements (although occasionally given to bouts
of self-doubt) and determined to make the company more cost
conscious. He is smartly dressed, has taken his jacket off to reveal a
crisply laundered, monogrammed shirt and sits at the head of the
table smoking a cigar; every inch the TV mogul.

Tony is tall, casually dressed and relaxed. He appears confident
in his own ability and has every reason to be so since his reputation
within the industry is very high. He is known to have a strong social
conscience (which he would deny), but is seen as a commissioner
and maker of quality programmes rather than a crusader. He does
not believe that the content of the programmes, their type, or the
scheduling of them is anything to do with Neville. He takes himself
to be responsible to him and, through him, to the Board for the
cost of them and holds himself accountable to his peers and,
ultimately, the Independent Broadcasting Authority, for the quality
of the material the company puts out.

Neville has called the meeting to 'find out' what Tony and his
team are doing with regard to programmes. Tony has toyed with
the idea of not attending but has decided to do so in order to clarify
some issues with regard to facilities. As we join them, they are
discussing 'SLAMM', a satirical programme which has made the
headlines before its first episode:

Neville: I gather from this that, quote, 'SLAMM made the *News
            of the World* and *The Sun* look tame', unquote; that it,
            quote, 'is taking on everyone, the Queen, the Royal
            Family, the Prime Minister, the Opposition, the Judges,

the Churches, the Unions . . .', unquote.
[*Tony, twisting his pencil and slumped in his chair, laughs quietly.*]

Neville: I don't know what it is you find amusing in all of this, Tony. I was asked about SLAMM the other day by the Chairman and I had to tell him I know nothing about it, other than it was over budget.

Tony: It's not down to him to know about it. Nor you, for that matter.

Neville: Oh, so I have to learn what TVN is doing from reading the newspaper, do I? Do I? How the hell am I expected to cope with questions when I don't know the first thing about what is going on? It sounds as though we are in for a rough ride on this one, if the papers are anything to go on.
[*He picks up the newspaper once more.*]
Quote, 'It is understood that the IBA has censored material which it took to be anti-semitic', unquote.

Tony: Untrue. Nothing anti-semitic about it.

Neville: No censorship then?

Tony: Didn't say that. They took it to be anti-semitic. It wasn't. Just a joke about pencil sharpeners. They insisted it came out.

Neville: What else had to come out, Tony?

Tony: Look, where is this leading us, Neville? It's my job to deal with the IBA and I'm doing it. Why don't we discuss something important, like why it is when I hire freelance producers, they can't find a bloody desk to sit at? Why is it that getting a typewriter around here is like extracting a bloody tooth?

Neville: I want to talk about programmes, Tony. As Managing Director, I am responsible for this company . . .

Tony: And I am responsible for its programmes. If you want to talk about them, how about talking about the awards we picked up last month? Two. Better than any other independent. Or the ratings, let's talk about the ratings. Three in the top seven last month. That brings in the advertisers, doesn't it? Let's talk about that . . .

Nevile: What about SLAMM, Tony, will that get an award? Let's
            talk about that . . .
Tony: Don't know. Like all programmes, it's a risk and I'm paid
            to take them.
Neville: And I'm paid to know about them.
Tony: All you need to know you can get from *The Sunday Times*.

Pretty powerful stuff, I think you will agree, and on the surface an interaction which you may well take to be an example of rebellion against authority. For me, it is much more an issue of autonomy. Tony is magnificently, even insolently, self-possessed. His independence, however, does not command respect; rather it intimidates others and, in particular, Neville. The Managing Director clearly needs his Programme Director more than the latter needs the former. It follows, and the extract demonstrates it, that Tony can afford to be indifferent to the needs of Neville; he refuses to play the game as defined by Neville and seeks to change it: let's talk about desks and typewriters. An autonomous individual stays cool when others make demands; Tony hardly bothers to rise to the challenge that Neville presents and does so only to the extent of brushing it aside: 'All you need to know you can get from *The Sunday Times*.' The comment is breathtaking in its arrogance, but Tony senses the imbalance in the relationship; Neville shows that he needs Tony much more than Tony needs him and, in so doing, puts the Programme Director in control.

This results in Neville making heroic efforts to provoke Tony into recognition of his, Neville's, position; a course of action which will only serve to reinforce Tony's sense of being in control, being the person around whom everyone must dance. Neville's frontal assault is partially successful in having Tony respond. Until this meeting, Tony simply ignored Neville's attempts to elicit information about the programmes in production. Indifference makes Neville angry *and* creates an emotional dependence that causes the executive 'team' to focus exclusively upon the interaction between these two actors. Only these two talk, everyone else is literally a spectator, each one of them powerless to intervene, none capable of resolving the pattern that emerges from this kind of interaction.

It is possible to speculate further around this matter of autonomy. What Tony is proclaiming, essentially, is that independence is good, to influence rather than be influenced is important and that to have little or no need for the approval of others is appropriate behaviour for a senior manager. His behaviour could be said to signal to others that being your own person is extremely important, that real power comes from self control; that responding impersonally allows others space and freedom and in a democratic society such behaviour is to be applauded. This may be clearer when we run the scene on a little.

Neville: Do you seriously think it appropriate that I should have to read about my own programmes in *The Sunday Times?*

Tony: That appears to be a problem for you but it is not for others, nor was it for your predecessor. I am the Director of Programmes – a fact which appears to get you hot under the collar.

Neville: I am the Managing Director – a fact which you refuse to acknowledge.

Tony: Not true, Neville, not true. I have no problems with you as MD. It is you who appear to wish to challenge my decisions as Programme Director.

Neville: Are you saying I have no say in programming matters?

Tony: Are you claiming that you do?

Neville: Of course. No one could imagine a company where the MD did not have a say in the product which goes out of the doors.

Tony: I can and this is it. You can and do legitimately influence budgets and costs. What actually leaves here – the shape, texture and quality – is my concern.

Neville: You are one of the most obtuse and exasperating people I have ever worked with.

Tony: I really cannot see that, Neville. I am doing my job which, apparently, you resent, and you are doing yours, with which I have no problem . . .

And so on. Neville is turned into a supplicant, please recognize my rights in this area, acknowledge me as a person, as your boss. He is, odd though it may seem, emotionally in Tony's grip and every interchange serves to underline this. Tony appears to be a more complete person than Neville, who appears desperate to assert himself; the more he demands recognition the less, paradoxically, he is likely to get and the more foolish he will appear to be. On the other hand, Tony's autonomy is destructive; it denies both his own and Neville's needs for maintenance. It works against trust and mutuality and promotes an atmosphere of antagonism which vitiates any sense of team work.[12]

I will conclude with a scene depicting what I have termed the struggle of the new. We are back on familiar territory with our old friends at Friction Free Castings, in the same room some months after our first encounter with them after Tom, the new Marketing Director, has been in post for a year. He has found his feet and is now seeking to revise ideas and procedures. This, occasionally, takes a challenging form as in this extract; Paul is once again addressing their failure to meet forecast:

Paul: So another month, another result not quite up to scratch . . .
Tom: Way behind, Paul. Way behind.
Paul: OK. Behind.
Tom: Way behind. A long way from what we should expect of ourselves.
Paul: Yes, but as we have heard from Tony and the rest, and from you for that matter, there are reasons . . .
Tom: I know, Paul. There are reasons. I've always more good reasons for not delivering than the rest of you put together, but isn't it time we took a clear look at what we are doing in these meetings? We are reassuring ourselves, that's what we are doing, reassuring ourselves when there is no good reason to be reassured.
George: Precisely my feelings. I keep saying it, we ought to be ashamed.
Tom: I am not ashamed, George, and neither are you when it comes down to it. I just don't want to go on time after time drawing false conclusions from the circumstance we find ourselves in. Something is very wrong. I have not met the targets, I am way behind, but everyone seems happy to accept my excuses. Don't worry, you've made a cock of it but you're a good chap really.
            [*There is a long silence. Paul stares across at Tom.*]

Paul: You want me to be openly critical of you then, do you?

Tom: I'm not sure I would like it and I am sure I don't *want* it but perhaps it's needed.

Tony: Not here, though – one-to-one in Paul's office, if it's necessary.

Tom: Why not here? Why not put it out on the table? You probably think it's down to me and I think it's down to you but we don't say so. At least not here in this room – in the bog, yes, at lunch, on aeroplanes, in cars, yes. But not here. Why not here? My competence is a matter of concern to you, yours is important to me, but we pretend everything is OK – we are all doing our best.

Paul: Well, I trust we are. This is not the place to air matters of competence. You are all competent, all good performers or you would not be here. Any criticism I have to make I'll make in my office. That's only fair, isn't it?

Tom is trying to break away from the old pattern, trying to change a way of behaving with which, until his interaction, everyone appears to have been happy. The script which obtains in this group, elaborated over the months and years of interaction, precludes other scripts developing. If, as appears to be the case, one is either reassured or proclaims shame, there is little room for any other improvisation unless one or, as in this case, both of these aspects are rejected or destroyed. Tom is declaring that he regards this pattern as unacceptable, that he, Tom, wishes to initiate a different script. This kind of demand challenges the authority of the group, it raises issues about who is authorized to do what. Can we allow any Tom, Dick or Harry to question or destroy that which we have so carefully moulded to our own needs and collective personality? On the other hand, members of the group may be dimly conscious of the unsatisfactory aspects of the solution they have arrived at between them; they may be vaguely aware that, in this particular instance, a reassuring script does little to redress the problems of the organization. Some, therefore, may be attracted to the idea of modifying their script, but repelled by the suggestion that one way of achieving this transformation is to open themselves up to criticism in front of their colleagues. Tom's initiative is at once an opportunity and a threat. The group can either move forward and, however temporarily, destabilize familiar patterns or they can reassert them by expelling his ideas; they can, and later actually do, make him a scapegoat, treat him as a pariah or deviant.

Tom is to be seen as doubly deviant; he is not only suggesting that the old pattern is fundamentally wrong, he is suggesting a new one which is extremely threatening. In a sense, though, if only it could be recognized, he is acting for the group; its survival depends upon both its stability and its ability to incorporate novelty. If members, as they do, reject the challenge, attribute deviance to one member, they also reject the possibility of creatively modifying or rewriting the script which currently obtains.

I have tried to illustrate in this chapter half a dozen aspects of improvisation around fraternity and authority. At the risk of appearing to state the obvious, I must repeat that labelling these patterns as I have is not making a claim that they are either the only variants to be observed or the most important ones. Nor am I claiming that all there is to be adduced from each is that which I have adduced. Mine is one interpretation, the selection of a particular emphasis; yours may well be different. I would, however, be disappointed if, whatever the differences we may have on matters of emphasis and labelling, you were not to agree that what *is* observable in groups such as these are matters of authority and fraternity.

What I have chosen to focus upon and what I choose to address in seeking to bring about change is informed by an idea of what an effective executive team would look like. Much of that is implicit in the comments I have made in this chapter; in the next one I will make my ideas explicit.

4   The Way of the World

The maintenance of the organization, as I have attempted to show in the previous chapter, is an extremely difficult process to bring off successfully. A large number of groups appear to become stuck in routines which not only are experienced as unsatisfactory by those directly involved, but are considered debilitating by the organization as a whole. The failure of the top team to get its act together has consequences for others:

> If the power center at the top is in chaos, what hope has the rest of the corporation for constructive action? Business cannot go on as usual. Limp, anxious and vulnerable, the organization is unable to react effectively to new threats. As the contagion spreads, even distant departments are soon infected with pettiness, personal rivalries linked to different leaders, and arbitrary rulings of little logic or importance.[1]

Each member of this group experiences a near constant dilemma. On becoming a member of the executive, each experiences (though none may actually be able to label the experience) an ambivalence about the group. *Simultaneously* they wish to be 'part' of the team and 'apart' from it. Thus each desires to be part of an effective whole, but, in fusing with others to achieve this, each fears a loss of individuality. George, it can be argued, wishes to be part of a successful executive team, but, in doing so, he does not wish to lose his Georgeness, that which he takes to be his separate and distinct self. Attraction to the group is accompanied by a fear of being swamped, of being taken over, rendered a cypher, neutered, castrated; remaining independent, on the other hand, triggers fears of diminishing influence, isolation, exclusion and rejection. This ambivalence – which I take to be part of the human condition – is periodically revisited throughout the life of each and every group. It is not a stage to be gone through; it underpins the entire process of interaction, more or less salient but always and everywhere the ghost at the feast.

Matters of authority also haunt the Boardroom table. George looks to Paul for 'firm leadership', but when he receives it (or a semblance of it), mutters darkly to himself and revels in a tone of injured innocence. 'Of course I wasn't going to do something at the Board meeting, what kind of fool do you take me for.' Again each member looks to others to receive or to give a lead, but each fears domination by a tyrant. Authority slips imperceptibly into authoritarianism; even as the former is demanded, the latter (into which the former has metamorphosed) is rejected.

These ambivalences are accompanied by considerable anxiety; emotion patrols the boundaries of such interaction with a cocked weapon. It is a matter of some feeling for George to strike out against what he takes to be the position of Paul and the rest of the group, but in doing so, not only they but parts of himself resist the action. His independence, he feels, risks destroying the group and must be contained, but his retreat simply tilts the balance the other way. He now risks being overwhelmed by the others and his anxiety takes on another form as a direct consequence; he can never win, nor can any other member of the group. Whatever he does, he is caught up in internal turmoil which he must contain lest it damage him and the others. He, like so many of the other executives we have listened to on the previous pages, is stuck in a routine from which there appears to be little hope of escape. He and the others are damned if they continue to behave in the manner to which they have grown accustomed, and they are damned if they seek to change it. It is particularly infuriating for George and his colleagues because their collective function is 'to reconcile conflicting forces, instincts, interests, conditions, positions and ideals', and it seems that because of these very forces, instincts, etc., they cannot even begin to address the task.

Trying to do something about the contradictions and ambivalences which constitute the group experience can often make matters worse. Let me illustrate what I mean by a further extract from the long running Paul and George show. This time it concerns Hugh – in charge of Product Development – who is not a frequent contributor to debate; indeed, for much of the present meeting he has been silent. Some of the time he has been observed to have his eyes closed. The rest are discussing objectives, more specifically the need to set them and share them.

Derek: It seems to me that we ought to make an effort to set them quickly . . . it's sense.

George: I'm a hundred per cent behind it. Hundred and ten per cent, if you like.

Paul: Alec?

Alec: Couldn't agree more. Tighten things up. [*Pause*] As long as we all do it.

Paul: OK. Let's do it, then.

Alec: We haven't heard everyone. Does silence signal agreement?

Paul: Who haven't we heard?

George: Derek hasn't declared his hand. Never does . . .

Derek: I spoke up before you, George . . . makes sense to me.

Alec: Tony hasn't declared.

Tony: Yes. OK. Nothing ventured, nothing gained. If you are all for it, who am I to say no . . .

Alec: And Hugh.

Paul: Hugh?

Hugh: What?

Paul: Are you agreeable to us sharing our objectives or not?

Hugh: I cannot see the point of having them if we don't share them, but we've been here before and nothing real came of it.

George: Come on, Hugh – stop wasting time. Are you in or out? If you are out, so am I – no point unless we all do it. Bloody typical, of course, we can never agree upon anything.

Alec: There's always one, isn't there?

Derek: Hang on, hang on. Hugh has a point, we have been here before and not delivered.

George: I knew you were not behind it . . .

Derek: It's not a question of not being behind it. I've said it's
           what we need, I'll go along with it, but Hugh has a point.
George: We all have a point but let's do something, for God's
           sake, instead of waffling on, qualify this, that and the
           other . . . we are in it up to our eyebrows, we need to do
           something, not sit around raking over what we have and
           have not done . . .

   The expression of differences is what the group is about, but
that very expression can threaten it. Attitudes such as those
displayed by Hugh are seen to prevent progress rather than as an
essential part of it. Nonetheless, when moves are made to suppress
him, Derek moves in to support him, only to find himself the focus
of attack. And so it goes on. As the group tries to overcome its
problems by beating dissent upon the head or excluding those who
will not conform, it actually stimulates the latent desire to be apart
present in each member; as this is manifested, it, in turn,
stimulates the need to belong. The more the group tries to
eliminate independence, the greater the pressure to assert it and,
of course, vice versa: the more assertion, the greater the pressure
to conform. It is as if, at some level or another, each member
becomes aware of the need for opinion and the emotions that
accompany its repression, but each is also fearful of the potential
schism from allowing any one simply to stand against the group.
   Everyone ends up feeling helpless. There does not appear to be
a way out. Some time later, an attempt is made to come to grips
with the feelings of helplessness:

Alec: We keep doing this, you know . . . getting caught in
           attacks and counter attacks on each other.
George: That's because we don't do anything.
Alec: We don't do anything, George, because we never allow
           ourselves to do anything.
George: That's just the point I am making. We don't do anything
           because we spend time talking about why we do nothing
           . . . makes your head spin, all this talk about talk. We've
           a business to run.
Alec: But how can we get to grips with it, if we don't look at
           what we are doing?

George: We are not *doing* anything. We talk about doing things – endlessly.

Tony: Round and round. Interminably. I'm with George. Let's do something – set some objectives, monitor them, what you like, but no more chatter, please . . .

This appears simply to compound the problem. The group cannot talk about the fact that it is stuck because it is stuck; it appears doomed to perform the same routine for ever; from within, there appears no way out. Every attempt to talk about the repetitious cycle invites a response which cues the next round.

Such circumstances are clearly not easy to change; the more one attempts to eliminate tension, the greater it becomes and the more determined members of the group appear to be to repeat their routines. To further understanding of how the patterns may be broken, I need to make explicit the dynamics which create 'good teams'. Much of what I have to say is, of course, implicit in earlier parts of the book; some of you will be there before me.

First, I will consolidate my position with what I take to be an axiom and follow it up with an assertion. The axiom: authority and fraternity are the referents around which a great deal of behaviour at executive level in organizations occurs. Given the amount of material I have presented, I take it that such a proposition commends itself to general assent. The assertion: each one of us is individually ambivalent towards membership of groups (executive or otherwise); we wish to be 'a part' of it and 'apart' from it, dependent and independent. Interactions in executive groups heighten these feelings of ambivalence since the purpose of such groups is to reconcile conflicts, instincts, interests and positions. To achieve such a laudable aim, members must commit themselves, must display the very differences that are to be addressed but, in displaying them, the group's capacity to function at all may be jeopardized.

Executive groups evoke strong feelings in most of their members. As the newspapers can attest, such groupings are particularly prone to dissent, splits and vituperative exchange.[2] Nonetheless, some groups seem to operate in a more consistent, coherent and productive manner than others; they appear to be able to contain the tension that arises from the ambivalences about membership and leadership that each member experiences. They do not do this by suppressing or denying these aspects of interaction; conflict and opposition appear to be necessary to the development of effective groups. What effective groups appear to be able to do is to both acknowledge and transcend ambivalences and differences. This is a difficult trick to pull off but one easy enough to recognize once it is seen or experienced. I will illustrate what I mean before going on to betray my oath to the magic circle by suggesting how one type of group may be transformed into the other.

Paul and his group are discussing the reorganization of the executive team; some members are to assume new roles and two of them, Tony and Eric, will, in future, only attend meetings when specifically invited. Having carefully outlined the proposals, Paul has asked for comments; everyone is working hard to listen:[3]

George: It seems sensible to me in that it allows us all to do what we appear to be best at . . . the executive can get to grips with the strategy and the operators can sort out the bottom line.

Derek: It seems a sensible split to me but I am not sure that I would like it were I to be in Tony's shoes. Or Eric's, for that matter. [*He looks towards both of them; neither of them catches his eye, neither volunteers an opinion.*]

Alec: It seems it will resolve some of our problems, particularly this constant struggle to separate out the day-to-day from the future. It will, no doubt, bring some other problems to the fore. How, for example, are we going to relate to Eric and Tony? How do we communicate the strategy?

Paul: Are you asking me? If so, I don't have an answer. I think it is something we have to resolve.

Alec: I feel a bit uncomfortable with that, we didn't devise the scheme, you did. I'm not sure I am keen to be held accountable for the implementation of something I had no hand in devising . . .

Paul: Say a bit more . . .

Alec: What?

Paul: Say a bit more about being excluded from planning the new structure.

George: It's your job to do that, isn't it? We are all interested parties, after all.

Paul: I accept that, George, but I'm not sure that invalidates the point I take Alec to be making. He is saying that I must bake my cake and eat it, if I take him right.

Alec: Am I? [*Laughter*]

Paul: OK. What are you saying, Alec?

Alec: I'm feeling a bit uncomfortable with this . . .

Derek: That's understandable, Alec, but I think it's an important issue. Paul wants to hear from us, he doesn't have to accept any of it but he wants to know where we stand. I'm with you – I had no hand in the design and feel I am being asked to dot the *t*s and cross the *i*s.

George: But can we do it? Is it possible for us all to put together a structure which involves us directly?

Alec: I'm not sure that is what I am asking for, George; I can't speak for Derek. I am simply saying I was not part of the design and I feel awkward, excluded – don't know what – about now having to rubber stamp it. Feels like a nonsense, really, decision precedes consultation.

Paul: If it feels like that to you, Alec, what does it feel like to Tony and Eric?

Tony: Do you need to ask? I feel a considerable amount of anger . . .

Two hours later:

Eric: I can see that and it makes sense, but I would ask that we all handle the circumstance carefully. It will not help matters if the rest of you go around saying in effect 'we are the masters now'.

Tony: I am not happy with it, as I have said at some length, but my unhappiness is more in what we may signal to others outside this group than with the aim of the change – to resolve some of our structural problems. I am content to go along with that – for the moment, at least.

Alec: I can live with it but we will need to be careful how we deal with each other. It seems like we have the beginnings of a new approach, let's give it a try . . .

Paul: I feel good about it, feel even better that we have all put our views on the table. It may not be absolutely the answer, as Alec says, but it's got the makings, it's got the makings . . .

The interaction here is of a very different temper to the material elsewhere in this book. There is disagreement here, there are clearly different positions taken up and different interests represented, but there is no sense of anyone being bludgeoned into submission. There is little sense of good triumphing over evil, there are no victors and vanquished, no heroes and no scapegoats. There is a certain mellow quality to the interaction, an autumnal feel, that is quite lacking in the other extracts used earlier. Rather than having the quality of crude melodrama, it has that of comedy: each member settling for 'a discriminated medley of the gratifying, the bearable, the upsetting, the grievous and occasionally the inimical.'[4] The comic stance implies a measured acceptance of the world, in all its fundamental disparateness. I say *measured* since reconciliation or accommodation to actuality includes acceding to a judgement as to what appears to be the best course of action. To acknowledge heterogeneity, disparateness and diversity is not to claim that everything goes, still less that anything does; movement occurs because of a sensed norm of what is appropriate. Simply because a group is prepared to listen to all points of view does not imply that they necessarily agree with them, nor does it imply that they will not be judged. An effective executive group exists, as Barnard was so keenly aware, to reconcile, that is 'to make [discordant facts, statements, etc.] consistent, accordant or compatible with' one another, but this does not allow for a ragbag of views, uncentred and unconnected. The group must include rather than exclude, but that does not deny it the proper concern to rationally discriminate between various perspectives. The paradoxical world of the effective executive group is both heterogeneous and normative.

I recognize that this ideal world I am depicting departs substantially from the more generally accepted views of effective executive behaviour. I recognize the fundamental ambivalence we all feel towards ourselves and to others, and do not wish either to suppress, to deny or to resolve it. An effective group, from my perspective, celebrates its ambivalence and its diversity; it positively revels in its acknowledgement of the way of the world and makes no grand claims to change it. What it does is provide a forum for a discussion of the problems which face it; a forum in which social actors do not flinch from the way things are variously seen to be; as one of Shaw's doctors in *The Doctor's Dilemma* puts it: 'The world isn't going to be made simple for you, my lad: you must take it as it is.'[5] Members of an effective executive team know the problems, know their own ambivalences and anxieties and do not expect to be able to completely resolve them. They can and do reconcile them, they feel they can 'push on' though failing in this or that project because they are free of illusions about what they can and cannot achieve. Effective executive groups are rarely characterized by the kind of doctrinaire singleness to which we are all prone at times; rather they are marked by the finding of a balance amid the contrarieties which are brought to their deliberations.

An effective executive group is one in which the members meet each other as whole persons; as neither a part of nor apart from the group but as both; neither dependent nor independent, but both. As I have sought to indicate, where one or other of these aspects dominates, where neither ourselves nor our colleagues can tolerate our ambivalence, we can do no better than establish an abortive, unbalanced or distorted kind of relationship. The effective executive group accepts its members as whole beings, as persons with ambivalent impulses and, in accepting them as such, allows space for each to come to working terms with other members. In an effective group, members are less concerned with themselves, since they can be open about their feelings and anxieties and more concerned with the task in hand. If I, as a member of such a group, can declare that I feel pushed into assuming a role with which I am profoundly uncomfortable, it is likely that neither I nor the group will become stuck in a routine which endlessly plays out my anxiety and unhappiness in a fashion we would all feel difficult to understand, leave alone address. Freed from the necessity to covertly or unconsciously handle or project my feelings, I can question my own actions. I do not, in such a team, have to say, like George, 'We are losing money, I am a shit, a no-good, reprehensible person, a moral delinquent', still less do I have to cast about me and say, 'and so are the rest of you'. Not being bound up with anxiety, costive with emotion, I can acknowledge error, I can note my own lack of competence and yours and 'push on'; I am not disabled by an inability to get everything right first time, or by what I see to be my own shortcomings, or by those of others. I recognize the way of the world, that events are shaped by men and women who are less than perfect and yet are not hostile to betterment. Reconciliation and accommodation – the end product of struggling, manoeuvring, twisting and turning, giving as well as taking – is made possible by the relative equality of each member of the team, the recognition and encouragement to act as whole persons.[6]

Such a posture is not common. As I have indicated, the usual response to ambivalence is to choose one pole or other and cling to it, rejecting that part of us which produces the greater anxiety. One can effectively withdraw from interaction with one's fellows; like Hugh, literally and metaphorically one can shut one's eyes to what is going on. Faced with the complexities which are the warp and weft of social and group life, the ambiguities of persons and things, one can run away, suffer a kind of defeat and throw one's hand in. Some do, withdrawing permanently from the fray; others of us withdraw temporarily, taking time out (we tell ourselves) the better to fight the next time.

On the other hand – and equally melodramatic – some decide to take on all comers; not afraid of power and leadership, but fearing dependence inordinately, they set out to take everyone and everything by storm. Such figures are now graced with the title of charismatic or transformational leaders and are seen as latter-day saviours. Theirs is the melodrama of triumph. It is frequently short lived, since the exercise of power on this scale is certain to arouse antipathy, censure, hostility and rejection. An overemphasis upon the control of others (whether or not it is claimed or accepted as being for the good of all – a dubious enough proposition) always and inevitably produces a reassertion of the opposite; the 'oppressed' or 'led' demand their right to go their own way. They may not do this by an overt act of rebellion, they may prefer satire, sabotage or dumb insolence, but whatever their means, however long it takes, those in whose name utopianism is promulgated will undermine it.

In organizations, as elsewhere, social actors need to steer a course between unrelenting conviction of their own (frequently individual) rectitude and the genial abdication of judgement. The effective executive group is characterized by members who neither proclaim 'my ideas or none', nor murmur 'just tell me what to do and I'll do it'. Extremes are to be acknowledged, but not accepted. They are to be avoided by members maintaining pressure upon themselves – pressure to avoid the excesses of a critical and attacking spirit (belittling the efforts of everyone), whilst simultaneously avoiding an uncritical adaptation to the way things appear to be by keeping in mind that things can be changed. An effective team recognizes the imperfections of the world in which it finds itself, of its own shortcomings, but can imagine and aspire to less imperfect states. The team which functions well is the one which maintains a tension between the idea of doing better and the sense of the way things inevitably are, the team which finds a mean between a hard utopianism ('management by objectives will turn the company around') and gross cynicism ('management by objectives is a do-it-yourself-hangman-kit').

Such a mean is essentially a comic one, a measured acceptance of what is and of what may be possible. It is not one commonly sought or observed in organizations where issues are rendered in much more melodramatic terms. Executives develop strategies, mount campaigns, set up task forces and blast the opposition. Comic acceptance is a language of peace; it implies adaptation, adjustment, accommodation, reconciliation, compromise . . . some very dirty words indeed if, as you may be, you are convinced of the value of assertive individualism. Tolerance you may just about be able to stomach, but compromise, falling into line . . . quick, give me back my copy of *Iacocca*. And you are wise to be suspicious. It is not possible to adopt the comic mean without running the risk of overdoing it, slipping to the position where anything goes. Yet the vocabulary of reconciliation (to stick to Barnard's terms for the moment) does not necessarily imply subservience or a reduction in human dignity. Rather it acknowledges the claims of others, it is democracy in practice (the curl of your lip as you read this will tell you something about your own willingness to accord equal rights to others), it is the gracious conceding that neither you nor anyone else has the prerogative on how to run any complex organization.[7]

Acceptance, the working towards a comic mean, is decidedly not a soft option. It requires that each of us forgoes the excitement of taking on the world in hand to hand combat, that we deny ourselves the luxurious sense of being the only one in step: seeing things not in the light of an absolute, but in the light of possibility. It is a coming together instead of a falling or flying apart; it is a prescription for a society in which we can coexist and, gradually, turn individual imperatives into the shared actions of common sense.

Rightly or wrongly, I want Paul and his colleagues to experience this brave new world; I want them to be reconciled and to be able to promote both a thorough exploration of their differences and a bringing together of their ideas. Given what I have said about the power of scripts, the routinization of behaviour and the difficulties that are experienced in seeking to understand what one is doing, leave alone revise it, how can I or anyone else bring about such a change? My position isn't quite that of other writers – that society is external to us, that it predetermines and predefines almost everything we do – but it appears perilously close to such perspectives.[8]

> Society, as objective and external fact, confronts us especially in the form of coercion. Its institutions pattern our actions and even shape our expectations. They reward us to the extent that we stay within our assigned performances.[9]

No one forces us to follow the scripts which we encounter, no one twists our individual arms; we enact the scripts because we have learned the lines and because we identify with the characters. We have developed a sense of who we are by casting inside ourselves an image of what we find as we learn our parts; we steal from other actors who, in turn, are but reflections of others. What we call our 'self', therefore, is a compound of interleaved performances. These performances are not mere trappings and shows, they are the real thing:

> It would, however, be missing an essential aspect of the role if one regarded it merely as a regulatory pattern for externally visible actions. One feels more ardent by kissing, more

humble by kneeling and more angry by shaking one's fist. That is, the kiss not only expresses ardour, but manufactures it. Roles carry with them both actions and the emotions and attitude that belong to those actions.[10]

Berger's ideas are a distillation and refinement of those put forward by George Herbert Mead, who, as I showed earlier, held that the self is a social creation, arising first of all in a dialogue of gesture, such as in a boxing match, for example, in which one combatant gets the message of the other's gestures and begins to plan future gestures such as a feint.[11] The genuine self, Mead argues, is born when the organism begins to put itself in the place of the other to see what its own behaviour may mean to that other: here is me feinting with the left, how will he see that, what will he do? From this primitive vocabulary of gesture, each of us derives our sense of self as an independent entity:

> In so far as one can take the role of the other, he can, as it were, look back on himself (respond to himself from) that perspective, and so become an object to himself. Thus again, it is only in a social process that selves, as distinct from biological organisms, can arise – selves as beings that have become conscious of themselves.[12]

The logic of the view is inexorable: whatever the 'impulse', an individual's actions are shaped and controlled by those around him (literally or metaphorically) and he or she is but a cipher, a nonentity, someone who exists as of no value except in association with others.

Such a view, of course, accounts well for persistence, but offers nothing to describe, explain or account for change. From such a perspective, anti-social actions are simply unthinkable, let alone unrealizable. I am no more, no less than the parts I play – a pawn rather than an origin:

> This view [role theory] tells us that man plays dramatic parts in the grand play of society, and that, speaking sociologically, he *is* the masks that he must wear to do so. The human person also appears new in a dramatic context, true to its

theatrical etymology (*persona*, the technical term given to the actors' masks in a classical theatre). The person is perceived as a repertoire of roles, each equipped with a certain identity.[13]

The essence of this perspective is, of course, neatly caught in Stoppard's play *Rosencrantz and Guildenstern are Dead*: 'Give us this day our daily mask.'[14]

There is a way out, an escape from the notion of Society as the great puppet-master. The seeds of it lie in the ideas of Georg Simmel, another of the great unread.[15] In an essay entitled 'On the Theory of Theatrical Performance', he goes well beyond simple notions of role playing:

> To play a part, not just as hypocrisy or as a deceit, but in terms of the involvement of the individual's life in a single expressive form which is entered upon in some pre-existing, pre-determined way, is part and parcel of the way in which our everyday life is constituted. Such a role may be appropriate to our individual self, but it is nevertheless something other than this individuality and not an intrinsic of its innermost and unitary being.[16]

Simmel goes on to argue forcefully that undertaking a role does not mean that one *is* that role; nor is it simply a game. 'It is not that we do these things (to which a civilized existence and our fate consigns us) only in a superficial way, but we unconsciously represent something which we, *in ourselves*, are not.' I want particularly to stress this point lest there be misunderstanding. This is not impression management, the art of the confidence trickster; what occurs when George is involved with his role as Finance Director is not simply effect, it is not a dishonest show; he and the rest of us are occasionally completely possessed by the parts we play.[17] Nonetheless, it is my experience that I am something more than the parts I undertake, indeed, that to varying extents I create these roles and write the dramas in which I perform. Not only is there an actor behind the role, there is also a dramatist who creates parts for himself/herself and others. Paul dramatizes George, 'I trust you are not.'; George dramatizes the rest of us, 'I find these figures totally depressing and completely unacceptable; I am surprised that no one else does. We all ought to resign!' There is hardly a scene in social life or dramatic art in which one character is not trying to dramatize another. Almost all of us at one time or another act at some moments like a playwright, employing a playwright's consciousness to impose a certain posture or attitude on another. To be sure, it is a matter of degree – some of us are fundamentally dramatists, some actors – but the point remains: it is possible to separate the playwright from the script, the actor from the performance. The fundamentally theatrical attitude I want to hang on to is a creative response to what life presents; yes, there are scripts, there are predefined social roles, but you and I are more than the dramas we enact. We are moulded by our experience which is unique; our lives consist in or are shaped by the events we participate in and the roles we play, but it is *we* who enact, *we* who channel our energies in a particular and peculiar fashion which makes them all our own. As Simmel puts it: 'An actor may perform many parts which both shape and are shaped by his innermost being.' Difficult though it may be to believe when you look around, all of us carry within ourselves the spark of creativity; we are painters, poets and actors.

> In the same sense, therefore, in which we are poets and painters, we are also play actors; i.e. culture endows every aspect of life with this characteristic. Without being in any sense false or hypocritical, the personal existence of the individual is metamorphosed into some pre-determined guise which is of course produced out of the resources of his own life, but is nonetheless not merely the straightforward expression of his own life. The possibility exists for us to assume such appearances, even strange ones, and neverthe-less remain consistent with our own nature. We are harnessed into this paradox at all times.[18]

Acting is not concerned with *reproducing* something but essentially with *interpreting* and *creating*; this is as true of social performances as it is of those found in theatres. I do not pretend that this perspective is original; it follows closely enough from the interactionist frame I elaborated in the previous chapter. We can be free from the apparent determinism of social forces, since these forces, all social realities, are artefacts. We write social life and, in turn, are cast for parts within it.

> Sociology, by emphasizing the 'fictional' nature of much social behaviour, provides the basis for seeing human behaviour as a 'construction'. It is not something immutably determined by 'human nature' or our genes. The hope exists that with greater knowledge, man can create social systems which offer greater opportunity for the full expression of human life and consciousness. He can modify the set of functions which surround him and bind him. But to do so, he must sense the possibility of escape.[19]

Consider for a moment what dramatists and theatrical actors do. Some of them do – it is true – hold a mirror up to nature, reflecting social forces and practices; usually with a purpose, to cause us – the audience – to reflect upon the practice we see laid out before us. Some, however, go beyond this and do not so much show us how we act in our present society, but create new possibilities for us; plays are not escapes from 'reality', but foreshadowings of the way things could be, ought to be. The work of the great dramatists shows us ways of escaping from the older and inadequate fictions which have been refined into systems. The notion of *plays*, related as it is to what appears to be an essential human characteristic, serves to reinforce my point. As humans, we create ourselves and our society through play and plays, fiction and novels, social scripts and improvisations, and in so doing demonstrate our capacity to be a self, to play, to dramatize, to make and remake.

Perhaps all of this can best be summed up by a paraphrase of Berger: 'Reality is socially constructed, socially sustained and socially transformed.'[20] Each of us performs in a series of repetitive routines, for the most part with skill and a degree of commitment and for much of the time without thought as to what it is we are about and why. Occasionally we are confronted with novel situations which demand that we behave consciously but, more often than not, our attention is limited to finding a familiar script which will fit the new circumstance; once having found it, we continue performing as before. Nonetheless, no two performances are the same; some performances we are committed to more than others, and all of the time in however rudimentary a fashion we are utilizing our capacity to interpret, create, dramatize, improvise and perform. Some of us some of the time are directly aware of ourselves as artists and in that awareness, however inchoate, lies the possibility of escape from the social forces which in less conscious moments we take as constraints upon our action. Oliver Goldsmith, an eighteenth century playwright, will serve to illustrate my point. His drama *The Good-Natur'd Man* is concerned with three characters, Lofty, Croaker and Honeywood, each of whom suffers from particular perspectives on reality. Lofty takes people to be more gullible than they are, Croaker is paranoid and Honeywood, prefiguring many a human relations specialist, holds that people, if treated with endless generosity and kindness, will respond better and better. After a series of trials and tribulations, in which the extremes of each perspective are exposed, the trio come to see themselves more clearly. Honeywood, for example, the sentimentalist, learns to spot and denounce his own overenthusiasm for benevolence. 'How have I sunk by too great an assiduity to please! How have I overtaxed all my abilities, lest the approbation of a single fool should escape me!' He learns as he goes broke that benevolence must be balanced by a degree of self-interest.

The point of this apparent digression is that, just as characters in plays can come to self-awareness, can be reconciled to the way of the world, so too can characters in real life. George can be brought to see the consequences of his actions, as can Paul, as can the rest of the group. Without some intervention, however, some precipitation of this learning such as occurs in the theatre, this realization may never occur. Indeed, the very 'stuckness' of their interactions may prevent it. What is needed is *peripeteia*, a change of fortune, a reverse of circumstances and/or a distancing of the actors from their roles. It is difficult to bring about the former, not easy to effect the latter, but more in the realms of possibility. Reversal and alienation form the bases for my interventions in groups such as that at Friction Free Castings.

The first step is to separate the social actor from his/her roles and performances; to insert, as it were, a sheet of perspex between the self and its enactments. George and his colleagues need a *metatheatrical* perspective if they are to understand what it is they are about and if they are to make some attempt to change it.[21] From within the theatrical frame, they can and do adjust their behaviour, they do things differently, but are unable to *transform* what it is they do since they lack any overall sense of themselves as performers, members of a system or whatever. It may help if I illustrate my drift with an example. The term 'method' denotes a particular scientific procedure; it is the specification of the steps which must be taken in a given order to achieve a given end. Methodology, although related to method, is, as it were, a concept of the next higher logical type. It is the study of the plurality of methods which are applied in the various disciplines; it has to do with the general activity of acquiring knowledge. One cannot, logically, talk about methodology from within the frame which constitutes method, but one can talk about method from within the frame of methodology; it is a *meta*method.[22]

George and his colleagues cannot address the intrinsically theatrical and dramatic nature of the interaction from within such a frame; to address such issues, they must step out of the frame, adopt a metatheatrical perspective, see themselves as performers which *qua* performers, of course, they are unable to do. Regarding themselves as performers is a very different state from performing. The theatre requires a suspension of disbelief, but to regard ourselves as performers requires a suspension of belief, a movement from what we take to be *real* life to regarding it as *make-believe*.

There are, of course, a number of ways in which this shift of perspective can be brought about;[23] I have written elsewhere about the means to alienate oneself from one's direct concerns and immediate environment. I do not intend to rehearse that list again here; rather, pursuing in part my notion of life as comedy outlined above, I wish to proclaim a role for fools in and around organizations. Not idiots, not people with funny hats and red noses (there is no shortage of clowns in organizations); rather jesters, dressed in motley with cap and bells – those who in other times and other societies have been termed 'wise fools'.

I will explain myself more fully in a moment. First, I offer a few comments upon folly and foolishness from a more general perspective. I will begin with a quote from Anton C. Zijderveld, a leading expert on folly:

For the duration of their mirthful performances, traditional
fools rejected the established patterns of thought and
emotion, the norms, values and meanings of daily routine, the
roles and habits of everyday life – in short, the structures of
the taken-for-granted lifeworld . . . They were strangers in
the most original sense of the word – in this world but not of
this world. Traditional fools played erratic games with the
primary foundations of human existence, with the basic
structures of the lifeworld, with the essential criteria by which
human beings manage to experience meaning at all. Turning
reality upside down, they rendered it, for the duration of their
performance, to chaos, to the forces of unstructured primeval
energy.[24]

There are some telling phrases in this passage: the rejection of
'established patterns', of 'habits of everyday life', of the 'structures
of the taken-for-granted lifeworld'. The notion that fools were
(and are) 'strangers' *in* this world but not *of* this world' is also
powerful and evocative; I like, too, the idea of 'erratic games' being
played with 'basic structures' and, in particular, with the 'criteria by
which human beings manage to experience meaning at all'.
'Turning reality upside down' also has appeal, although I confess
to an element of anxiety around the fool's attempt to render it
chaotic. Folly is the 'logic of transition', the method of structuring,
seeking to routinize the unstructured and the chaotic by turning
that which was (and may still be) upon its head, seeking to provide
a means for verbalizing that which, in normal circumstances, is left
unsaid and may be unspeakable.

For those of you wondering why you picked this book up, let me
push you a little further. I am arguing that life, organizations,
institutions, societies assume foolish features as they move from
the 'old' to the 'new'. There are periods in our lives and in those of
our institutions which lack taken-for-grantedness, stability, continuity, order. It could be that the 'new' will be better than the 'old',
that we will experience the 'different' as more rewarding than that
to which we are accustomed, but there is always a risk, always a
degree of anxiety that change will be for the worse, a fear that we
(or our institutions) will be overwhelmed by anomie. Those who
lived (or live) in a traditional society were as much aware of the

inherent marginality of human and social existence and recognized that folly frequented life as much as order. To cope with it, they ritualized transitions and held the fool in high esteem. The traditional fool was not a lunatic, or an idiot; he (there were no female fools) represented the world of transition, one foot in no man's land, one foot in what may be.

Folly, from this perspective, is not something apart from reality; it surrounds it, marking out the boundaries of the normal, the taken-for-granted, the routine and the rational. Folly serves to reinforce the dominant values, norms and roles of society by, for a brief moment, sharing the obverse; order is reinforced by reversing it. Equally, and for our purposes more importantly, folly manages to demonstrate the very contingency of order by showing us that what we have, that which we take for granted, assume to be normal and necessary, could very well be different.

> The traditional fool contributed to the grounding of tradition – the values, norms and meanings of something – in the consciousness of individuals, yet by his contrary behaviour in which standard roles and hierarchies of power and authorities were reversed, he demonstrates to the members of his audience that things as they are could just as well be quite different, that reality as it is experienced in the routine of daily life can be transcended to a time from which 'normal' reality suddenly looks 'abnormal'.[25]

It is this ability to invert order, to cause the natural to be estranged, that I want to claim as a key feature of effective change agents; folly should be part of their repertoire, foolishness their stock in trade.

There are other parallels. The fool's relation to authority and fraternity is of note. The fool was a marginal man, unimpressed by authority (although clearly capable of being subdued by power).[26] In society but not of it, he was not likely to be caught up in the kinds of ambivalence I outlined earlier in this chapter. Authority was always met with 'mocking remarks and irreverent antics'. Power they respected, but attempts to give it the trappings of justification and legitimacy they regarded with scorn and sought to puncture. The fool was never (and is never) impressed by the outward show of authority; he was no respecter of office or of the game by which courtiers deferred to the definitions proffered by their rulers. The fool was ever likely to pierce the fine clothes and elaborate rules of decorum to expose the 'reality', the 'unpleasant nakedness of power'.

Nor was the fool a joiner. He stood alone, a member of no fashion, with no allegiance other than to his master and that of the most paradoxical kind, bound to him by a licence to continuously challenge the bond. Fools did not form parties, act as leaders of cabals or head up rebellions; they were disliked by many, shunned by all but a few and feared by most.

Consultancy may be seen as a piece of foolishness. Like our predecessors in cap and bells, we seek to make the familiar strange, to reverse the order of things such that what is taken-for-granted appears slightly, very slightly ridiculous. Like them, we may be prepared to question if not jeer at authority, keen to show it for what it is and what it could be. Like them, we are, or should be, marginal creatures, inhabiting the half-light between the organization and the environment, in it but not of it; we are liminal, persons of thresholds and transitions, occasionally involved in the action, but more often than not doing little more than offering a commentary upon it.

The juxtapositioning of a change agent and a fool is something more than a nice conceit. At times of change, what is needed beyond all else is foolishness, a willingness to play with reality, to consider as openly as possible a range of behaviour some of which, in other circumstances and other times, might be dismissed contemptuously. The fool may have no solutions, but he does invest transitions with a kind of residual magic, an ambiguity which heightens the excitement, the feeling that this time it might be different.[27]

By now, some of you will be objecting strongly to the line of this argument; I appear to be claiming that folly occurs at times of transition, that it is the special prerogative of fools who, whilst their activities may reveal the contingent nature of reality, have no aims beyond that of playing and whose activities nearly always result in a restitution of the status quo. Furthermore, I appear to be embracing such a role for myself: someone with a particular relation to authority and fraternity who 'reveals' the scripts which

underpin performances in organizations and is content to do just
that, leaving 'rebellion' and 'reform' to others. Just so. Or nearly
so. Wearing my cap and bells, I can and do provide the opportunity
for others to reflect upon the nature of their interactions, I hold a
mocking mirror to their institutions and practices. In my other
clothes as dramaturge, I can and do help those wishing to change
to rewrite their scripts. Unlike the traditional fool, my aim is never
simply amusement, I am more than a *homo ludens*, although,
arguably, I am of more value as a fool than as a dramaturge. In the
next chapter, I will outline how I go about my folly, how I create the
'marvellous dream' by juxtaposing the way of the world with the
way it might be.

> Then I dreamt a marvellous dream; suddenly, as I stood
> there, I was wafted away by the goddess of Fortune, who
> brought me all alone into the land of longing and made me
> look into a mirror – the Mirror of the World – saying, 'Here
> you can see untold wonders – all the things you most long for
> – and reach them too, perhaps.'[28]

5   Playing the Fool

The Boardroom of Friction Free Castings once more: a grey November afternoon, the cast as before. Having interviewed fifty senior managers, waded through pages of minutes and reports and sat in on a dozen or so meetings, I am reporting back to the group. Some are apprehensive, since they and their subordinates have provided some of the data I am presenting. For the most part, it is received in silence; Alec and Derek spend a great deal of time making notes. Paul, who has had a preview of the material, is watching reactions. I have begun with general issues about the nature of the business, matters of broad objectives and, somewhat nervously, I am gradually moving on to issues of immediate concern to those present in the room. The method is to quote directly without attribution from the interviews; the build up of comments is deliberate, but reflects the balance of views honestly:

> It's not pulled together well. It's not led very well. It's easy to criticize and it's easy to say that the lot at the top are all so bloody bad . . . but there is very poor coordination between different parts of the business. Alec does not talk to Tony, Hugh to Derek – we don't manage the business well at all.

> Clearly, there's too much freedom. We all go our own way because it's impossible for us to agree anything different.

> I'm not sure that we ever reach a conclusion. I am critical of the time we spend together. I am sure a very thorough job of analysis is done and as a result the final conclusions ought to be very good but we are bleeding to death in the meantime. I don't know that we can afford the time to go through all of

this with such a fine filter but we do, we refine and refine and never decide.

The simple fact, as I see it, is we've got too much capacity as a company and we don't make any decisions to reduce it, because whenever we do, there's always someone who is going to object. Alec in the UK, Tony in France and so on. So we avoid it, we 'look at it again' – and still do nothing.

I think when you talk about being strong, I think I'd like to talk a little bit about what I mean by strong, because I'm not sure that it's being a hard man or a bully. It does seem to be this ability to complete the final stage of a piece of analysis which leads through to a very fairly based decision, properly implemented. And applying that approach of analysis, review of options, decision making and implementation to the problems the group deals with, and that's what I mean by being strong – being firm in sticking to a process for making decisions. And being firm in sticking to what these decisions are. So I am not talking about a hard man or a bully or a red-faced, bull-necked guy, but a guy who goes through that logical process and then is concerned that the answer he has is the right one and has the strength of character to stick to it. I see elements of that decision making capability around, but I don't see all that ability combined in one man.

All right, let's ... OK, let's hope that Paul, George, Alec, Hugh and those supporting them have a fairly clear idea about where we are going and what to do next and why, and where our survival lies. And what we really ought to do and why it is we ought to get out of Spain or France or whatever – out of lawnmowers, for that matter ... and I bet they don't. I bet there is no agreement at that level.

If I am honest, we will have problems with running Friction Free whatever the structure, because of the nature of the people, and particularly of Paul Jenkins. Very nice chap, good engineer, heart in the right place, extremely hard working, got a grasp of an enormous range of things, but in his personal style, has great difficulty in disciplining himself and therefore in disciplining the organization.

This place could have worked. As you know, you can work almost any structure – depending on who's heading the people. Paul is out of his depth.

He has an amazing capacity to cheer people up, I don't know how he does it. Paul should be more authoritative. He is too cheerful, too nice. He cannot bear to hurt people or offend them or upset them and he bloody well ought to. If he upsets me, OK, I will curse him, but at the end of the day really, that's what I want.

In some senses, he is an excellent leader. But I would prefer to have someone who added to his talents by saying at the end of the meeting: 'OK, well, what we're going to do is this.' Now I don't really mind if, in agreement, we've agreed to go left . . . I wouldn't mind if the leader then said, 'We are going 90 degrees right. I've heard what you guys have to say, taken it into account – thank you very much. But like it or not, I have to take the rap for this and I'd be glad if you'd support me because if you don't, you are out of a job. And we are going right.' Now, Paul does not do that.

I put all of this down to the very ineffective monitoring of what is happening on the part of the executive. Let me say this – it has been a constant surprise to me that as an executive we do next to no monitoring of the serious business issues. There is no monitoring of Alec's business, none of Tony's, none of Eric's. None of them reports on major contracts, no feedback on decisions taken or not taken. Nothing. We collude to keep each other in the dark.

We'll only make progress when we get rid of an organization in which our immediate colleagues are actually the people who are running it day to day.

But the biggest problem, to get back to the crux of the organization issue, is that we have general managers debating round the table and making decisions about things that they have personal commitments to, very direct and very, very personal commitments, and it's nonsense, utter nonsense, to expect Tony Gent or Eric Wragg to make decisions which involve cutting off large chunks of their business. This sort of set up we have at the moment is great when things are really going well, everybody's expanding and you've got to make a decision whether to expand in that area or that area, but everybody is expanding, it's just a question of whether . . . some will grow faster than others. And that's great because some people are quite happy just to have a nice steady growth rate. But when things are flat, bearing in mind that last year we declined by 13 per cent, we've declined by about 50 per cent over the last three to four years, and 13 per cent up to last July, and in that situation I can't see how you can get any general manager sitting round the table making a positive decision about doing anything. Because it's going to be at the cost . . . somebody's going to have to suffer.

But my view is that, in the present situation, our sort of woolly consensus style of management, plus getting general managers to debate about the action that needs to be taken, is totally inadequate for our present situation.

There is an assumption that everybody is equally competent. I'm not certain that's true. But I think there is a thing around that everybody is – how can I express it? – let's say that competence is not often taken into account when assessing the views expressed by people.

You often get some poor devil who's all on his own – or maybe he's got one other person supporting him, and there's a quick flip round saying 'Well, does anybody feel strongly about this?' – no answer, and that's the end of it. Because it is a sort of eight to two thing, which does not necessarily take into account that those two, in terms of that issue at least, are highly competent, and do know what they are talking about.

It's a great shame because I feel that the people there are quite capable of participating in a good debate and arriving at a conclusion. There's always one or two that are a problem but . . . Of course, I don't think we know how we should behave. We've never had that debate. The things that are said . . . 'Come on – let's be completely open with each other, we shouldn't have any secrets from each other' – all that sort of talk, but when you behave in that way then you either tend to get excluded from the decision making groups or it can be worse in that your card has been marked as a trouble maker, or something. So, we are inhibited, not surprisingly.

Rarely a meeting goes by without at least one incident of some sort where one or other of us has said something which the other feels is a criticism, so has to be responded to.

Paul made his point very clearly, strongly known straight away, it was 'Off with George's head', wasn't it? 'I'll get somebody who will tell me good news with the same figures.' It's difficult then to pick it up, really.

I think Paul does influence it greatly. If it is known that Paul has a particular view on a particular subject, I think a lot of the members would go along with that. Alec would influence it to a certain extent, although I believe that from time to time Alec would have difficulty because Alec is Alec and is seen to be analytical and influencing Paul too much. I think a number of people would go against Alec in order to contain him.

I don't see him being good at that – he's a nice guy, I'll go out for a drink with him, but I see him as the wrong leader at this point in time for what needs doing. So I haven't got confidence that he or that group of people will actually . . . if all the strategy work was done 100 per cent perfectly and finished by Christmas, I wouldn't have confidence that that group of people would pick it up, make the right decisions and implement the right decisions. Hopefully, that's wrong.

Alec sounds very tough on a number of occasions and says all the right things, but I've known a number of examples where he's had difficult things to implement and he will back off for a long time, even years, because it's difficult. I think he can find reasons – I'm sure we all do it to an extent, depending on where we are, we can get away with it more or less, but the nearer you get to the top of the pile, the less you ought to be allowed to get away with it because you've got to be able to implement the nasties, in a decisive speedy way.

I think that some of the problems are the people we've got there. George is another one. Ought to be influencing greatly as Finance Director of such a company. I don't have confidence that George is going to lead us forward. I think that's one of the problems. It's easy to say . . . strike them all off and start with a new batch. But looking through the guys we've got, they . . . I haven't got confidence in them.

The likes of Eric and Paul and Tony Gent, I don't think many people would rate them very highly. I think they'd be disappointed in them and not confident that those guys would lead us forward.

One of Paul's characteristics is that he doesn't welcome people saying things that he does not want to hear. And he does punish them. I think Paul has favourites and he rewards them, and if you're not so favourite, he punishes you.

I think Alec has been influential, but he's tended to be too influential. And therefore there's a backlash. Don't know about Hugh. But on the basis that the most influential bloke in the company was the last bloke to talk to Paul, the people around here are most frequently the last people to talk to him. And therefore I would say they were the most influential.

Unfortunately, of course, when Paul behaves in a certain way to an individual, then a whole lot of other people join in.

I don't know why Paul does it. It's not malicious.

He's an autocrat at heart and he makes up his mind that he's right and then gets the group together to bring it to that conclusion as quickly as possible. Don't spend the time in debate. Just a different way of operating. The other problem is the lack of sensitivity to the need to get the group properly constituted and working together properly . . . He's said to me that it's a good group he's got and he sounded as though he meant it. He said 'It's a good group, works well together, no politics.' Well, I don't think it's a good group, I don't think everybody ought to be on it that is on it. We certainly don't work together. Not given the opportunity to work together. Probably could work together with a good deal of time and effort, and to say there are no politics, he must walk round with his eyes shut. Tripping over the politics every day.

A decision stands for as long as it's convenient, which is different to saying that it stands for as long as it's valid.

There is a problem, I feel, once Paul expresses a very strong view about something, such as 'We cannot let this happen. We must go. We must have this business' etc. I and others, others probably more than me, find it very unwise to argue too strongly against that.

There's no doubt that it's not difficult to build up a reputation for being awkward. It's not difficult then to get excluded from all these decision making groups, and so on.

Each one . . . when you go around, each director has his own hobby horse, personal commitment, and you can't have a proper discussion. Even if you do have a discussion and something is agreed, it doesn't happen, because the only person who can make it happen is the person who's in charge and he's got the commitment not to do anything, to leave it as it is.

Yes, good working relationships. People are relaxed and can talk to each other, but we do agonize about the situation. If you go and talk to Tony, he'll agonize about Alec's business, and if you go to Alec, he's agonizing about Tony's . . . It's always somebody else's business, this is the thing that's so ridiculous . . . all prepared to do something about somebody else's business but nothing about their own. So the first thing that happens, it's always predictable, anything about France, no matter what it is, Tony will defend it to the last ditch. Of course he will, he's defending his own.

One thing I do feel about Paul is that he is very approachable. I feel at ease in his presence.

And I hear, at senior level, comments about who said what at a meeting and you never guess . . . what a fool Mr So-and-So made of himself. And that type of politics I find very difficult to deal with.

I get so frustrated when somebody suggests that we spend some time reviewing how in fact we spend our 1000 hours a year of executive time in meetings, to be told 'Well, we looked at that five years ago, didn't we? I've still got the report gathering dust in my cupboard.' That to me is the comment of somebody who isn't a well rounded executive, who says things like 'We've got to stop worrying about this group thing. We've got to get and do the job we're paid to do.' If we spent more time being effective as groups within this structure, then I believe the structure would work more effectively. It's the people. I guess that good people can struggle in a bad structure, but people who aren't aware exactly what's going on in a questionable structure is a recipe for confusion.

I think this organization loves initiating things, they love analysis, they hate doing anything with the analysis other than preserving the status quo and they will find a logic for not changing things. And I can predict that that will be the outcome of this work as well. We will be honest with you; you will feed it back. We will do a lot of work, we will stand the world on its bloody head to get the work done, we will present it and arrive at a rational set of recommendations, and then agree why we can't do anything.

I put my notes down; there is more, much more, but I sense that there is little point in continuing. Most in the room are avoiding eye contact with me and none makes contact with his colleagues.

'So that's it', I conclude, 'stage one, a review of what you and your colleagues think about you, your colleagues and your organization. A reflection, a mirror of what the most senior group feels about being here.' I pause, rise, collect the notes, and going to the other end of the table, fill a glass and drink. I sense my pulse racing. I wait for someone to speak. Eventually someone does.

'Well, we ought to be ashamed of ourselves, we really should be. If that's us, we all ought to resign.'

Good old George. We are off and running.

There is, of course, nothing particularly foolish about this kind of feedback; true, the material is, in many cases, personal and potentially confronting, but it is the stuff of many an organizational change assignment. Folly in the sense I have attempted to describe it, a lack of a regard for authority and the present order is, however, essential to this stage and to the work which immediately precedes it. The views expressed in this meeting (which were, of course in part those of people seated around the table and, although cloaked in anonymity, their disclosure had been sanctioned by them), had been presented to Paul prior to the meeting, at which point a heavy demand had been made upon my own reserves of foolishness.

Paul was surprised by what he initially termed the 'intemperate' nature of the opinions given to me by his colleagues. He claimed to be 'disappointed in them', the implication being that somehow they had not lived up to his expectations of them, that holding such views was immature, unreasonable, even perverse. When confronted with the material, the sheer volume of it caused him considerable disquiet; he was visibly agitated and began to try to guess who had contributed particular views. He moved from disquiet to anger; how could they think that of him, he was working all hours under the sun for their good. He paced the floor, banged his hand upon his desk at moments of extreme irritation and, eventually, spent time gazing out of the window, before turning to me with a renewed determination:

Paul: OK. That's what you have picked up. Gossip. Uninformed opinion, tittle-tattle. Nothing to do with the business. Does not help anything . . .

Iain: Quite true, Paul, quite true. The fact that many of your senior managers have little or no sense of the direction the company is heading in, that most of them do not know what their priorities are, that they express a lack of faith in you and the executive group – gossip. Pure, uninformed tittle-tattle of little or no consequence . . .

Paul: But it is nonsense. Nonsense. I had them all together, not six months ago. At Tewkesbury. I told them all what we were aiming for and what our priorities were. They *know* what we are trying to do . . .

Iain: What you told them at Tewkesbury, Paul, is what you always tell them – that everything is OK really, that we are in a spot of trouble but, trust me, we will get out of it.

Paul: We will, we will . . .

Iain: How, Paul? You always say that. They see you, I see you, as the man who denies that there is a real problem and prevents me or anyone else flagging up the facts . . .

Paul: Christ, that's worse, isn't it?

Iain: George repeatedly points out that we are in a financial mess and you repeatedly tell him to shut up.

Paul: But it is not a crisis. He makes everything a crisis – we are not in a crisis – I've see it before – it's a hiccup; we will be out of it in months – a downturn, not a crisis.

Iain: What's this, then?

Paul: What?

Iain: This, that you are doing now. You seem to be denying this as well. Telling me that they have it wrong – their views are not what they have expressed to me . . .

Paul: But it's all one way. Things are not that black. Ask anybody what he thinks and he will complain, provide gossip . . .

Iain: You are trying to do to me what you do to everyone else. Tell me that I have it wrong – that I ought to think differently. That fifty-odd senior people, including members of your executive, do not believe what they are saying to me.

Paul: If they believe it, they are wrong. We do know where we are going, the team does work well together . . .

Iain: There is a Father Christmas and there are fairies at the bottom of the garden . . .

Paul: Look, I'm not sure I like being treated to your sarcasm, I am not sure we are going to get anywhere . . .

Iain: I am sure that you do not like it. Whoever said that you would? You hired me to do a job for you and I am doing it. Part of it is to cause you to look at things. If that takes sarcasm, so be it. A great number of people, senior, serious, committed people express an 'opinion', an overwhelming opinion that there is something wrong, they risk being specific and you deny it. In my view, you are doing the very thing they accuse you of – closing your eyes to bad news, desperately seeking the silver lining. There is nothing to be gained from that, and if it takes a bit of sarcasm to shake you out of it – good.

Paul: I don't find it very productive, that's all. It's a put down and, at the moment, I can do without it.

Iain: So can I.

Paul: What?

Iain: Being put down. I collect this material, talk it through with you and you deny it, practically accuse me of inventing it.

Paul: I did not. Do not.

Iain: How do we move forward, then? What we have are the *perceptions* of your managers about the company, about themselves, about you. They may or may not have it 'right', they may not be the 'facts', but their opinions and perspectives do influence what they do. If they believe they do not have clear priorities, they will act as if they do not.

Paul: You don't have to push it harder. You are right. I might not like it, but it is what they think and I have to face up to that

. . .

It would be simplistic to think that this was the breakthrough, the point where Paul acknowledged that there was a substantial number of problems which needed to be tackled, the point when he gained some insight into his own behaviour. Like many such events, it was followed shortly by a reversion to his previous position; a denial of the data and a flight into what I took to be the never-never-land of 'things-are-not-so-bad'. Such a retreat, of course, is understandable and I offer the scene not as any demonstration of Paul's obtuseness or idiocy but as an illustration of the kind of folly that is necessary to reveal the contingent nature of things. Paul has a momentary glimpse that what he does to others may lead to the opinions of him that he so much wishes to reject. Later, much later, in the conversation he is clearer about his role in denying others the space to put a contrary and 'negative' point of view:

Paul: OK. I accept it. That's what they think and I can see how they think it. The point now is to get out of it. Sort it out,

get everyone to think positively, move the company along
...

Iain: How will they know you accept it, Paul, whatever it is?

Paul: I'll tell them. I'll say we have talked. You have told me everything. You have, haven't you? You are not holding something even more dreadful back, are you?

Iain: No.

Paul: Well, I'll tell them I've heard it. I accept it. I can understand how they feel like that and this is what we are going to do to sort it out.

Iain: How will that help, Paul?

Paul: Help what? We have to sort it.

Iain: Sort what?

Paul: The problem. Poor morale, lack of direction, all that stuff we have been going on about for the past three hours.

Iain: That is not the problem. The problem is your unwillingness to let anyone express a contrary opinion, the problem is sharing definitions with people and developing shared solutions. If you simply tell them, 'I've heard what you've said to Iain. I accept it, this is what we are going to do', how will that help?

Paul: We have to do something positive.

Iain: The most positive thing you can do is to explore the negative.

Paul: Explore it?

Iain: Acknowledgement is not sufficient. It's like saying, 'OK, George, I hear you now – this is what you should be thinking.'

Paul: That's unfair. I accept that I deny others the ground but I am accepting their view here.

Iain: From me. Not from them.

Paul: You mean I should go in and invite them to say more about the problems? Invite them to put it all on the table? Own some of these comments?

Iain: It is a risk but it would be a clear demonstration in action that you are prepared to tolerate, even encourage, a thorough exploration of problem areas before proposing a solution.

Paul paces the room for a few minutes.

Paul: So I have to listen to this stuff again and encourage more of it?

Iain: Yes.

More pacing of the floor.

Paul: If I understand you right, you are telling me that my style is to move people on before they are ready? To block their expression of dissent and substitute my own view which they don't necessarily agree with?

Iain: In part, yes.

Paul: So in this particular case – these views you have collected – it will be more of the same if I just say, 'Heard it. Here's what we do.' They will not be convinced that I have really taken it on board?

Iain: Probably not.

Paul: I am not sure that I have. If I am honest, at least part of the time we have been talking, I have been wanting to move on – get on to something positive.

Iain: Let me try something out on you, Paul. A number of the comments are prefaced by the fact that you are a nice chap, good person to have around . . .

Paul: That's positive, at least.

Iain: Could be. Could also be one of the issues. Could be that you are so keen to be seen as a nice chap that you do not let any negatives arise – keep everybody sweet, don't let conflict emerge and everything will be OK – trouble is, that approach seems to result in the opposite – things are not OK and no one can tell you because you will not, cannot or do not wish to listen.

Paul agreed to a meeting with his most senior group and, eventually, went on to meet others who had provided the feedback and explored with them the issues they had raised. He found the sessions difficult and had to work very hard to suppress a tendency to proffer solutions before opinions and views long suppressed were exposed. Nonetheless, the change in his approach was very marked and the consequence obvious to him and every one else. In a sense, he became his own fool, inviting others to challenge his authority, to assert how the world looked to them and, in so doing, to reveal how they might like it to be. On the final occasion, after a stressful meeting with a group of managers who were particularly disaffected, he turned to one of his colleagues on the executive group who had been with him on the event to say:

Paul: It's a paradox, isn't it – the more negative you allow people to be, negative in my terms, the more positive the entire thing turns out to be.

To this point, I have concentrated upon folly on a one-to-one basis which, whilst not easy, is a different matter from folly in a group. Many of the problems I have delineated in this book are matters of relationships within executive teams, issues of authority and fraternity, and it is to this that I now turn.

To illustrate, let me remind you once more of the interaction which occurred between Hugh and his colleagues with regard to the strategy for product development. You will recall that Hugh 'owned' that his views on product development were diametrically opposed to those of his colleagues, notably Alec's, and furthermore 'admitted' that he had suppressed his opinions for some months even within the team which was now supposed to be working well together. My part in this event had been to talk to Alec, Hugh and Tom about the apparent inability of the Product Review Committee to come forward with proposals to rectify what many saw as inadequate product performance. In talking individually with members, it was clear that there were a number of issues that were giving members of the subgroup some problems. Hugh was the designated chairman of the committee, but Alec supplied the planning expertise and the planners continued to report to him, which in the view of some led to Alec covertly controlling the agenda and the members. One or two of the members thought that Alec wished to formally assume the chair and push his ideas, whilst others thought that Hugh was doing a good job in difficult circumstances. Hugh believed that Alec's view of the process of product development was fundamentally wrong, but had not confronted his colleagues with this perspective. Alec suspected that Hugh held a different view, since the latter's engineers 'clearly make no effort to follow an agreed strategy. They still work as if every project were equally important.' Each member was frustrated with each other and with Paul, who each in turn saw as not supporting their particular perspective. I put it to each that if he persisted in not discussing his differences with his colleagues, matters could only become worse. They agreed to meet and declare their positions; I prepared no papers, offered no data or interpretations; it was to be up to them to surface the problems and resolve them. Unfortunately, before this meeting had taken place, the matter became public in the wider executive team:

Hugh: I am not sure that I agree with that.

Alec: What?

Hugh: The need for an explicit document setting out target dates for new product development.

Alec: But that's the basis of our entire strategy.

George: It's what we agreed to months ago. You and Alec spent days putting it all together. Every customer, every product, line by line . . .

Paul: Just a minute, George – let's hear what Hugh is saying before we start in on him.

George: I'm not getting at him . . . I just want to understand what we have all been doing these past few months.

Alec: What are you saying, Hugh? That we have all been wasting our time because you didn't really go along with what you agreed?

Derek: That explains why we never seem to have proper product review meetings.

Paul: Hang on. Hang on. Hugh . . . [*invites him by gesture to contribute*]

Hugh: Well, it's just that I have reservations, that's all. Can't subscribe to this notion of everything being planned . . . customers don't work that way. Product development isn't like that – you spend time with your key customers and gradually something emerges. We are behind on all the dates specified.

George: By you! By you!

Hugh: By us, George by us and, yes, I had a hand in it. I went along with it but I am telling you now I do not believe that is the way to go about it . . . It doesn't happen like that. You cannot deliver new products to order. Look at the money we have been throwing at the 230, and what can we show for it? Nothing, or virtually nothing. To be sure, there could be a market for it if we had it but we haven't, and meanwhile we neglect the areas that we have established products in . . .

[*He tails off. There is a long silence, eventually broken by Alec in a tone of quiet accusation.*]

Alec: But you went along with this, Hugh. You were responsible for implementing the strategy. A strategy you disagreed with.

Hugh: That's correct. But you have to remember where we started from . . . We were in no position to agree anything, we had nothing going for us a year or so ago. Something agreed, even this, was better than nothing.

George: But it's fundamental. If you did not agree at the time you should have said so.

Hugh: I did on several occasions. Probably not strongly enough . . . then I went along with it. And ever since then, we have all avoided talking about our lack of progress – me included.

Paul: Until today.

Hugh: Until today.

It is clear from this extract that Paul is working hard to give Hugh space to own his position; it is equally clear that George and one or two of the others find this ownership at best tardy. They attack furiously:

George: Marvellous. Week after week we have gone on thinking we are all of one mind, now suddenly all bets are off.

Derek: We have spent hours on this strategy, days, weeks, *months*, only now to discover that the prime mover doesn't believe in it.

Iain: What are we trying to do now?

Derek: We? I don't know what you are trying to do, but I am angry with Hugh and I want him to know it.

Iain: Makes you feel better, does it?

Derek: As a matter of fact, it does. You asked us some months ago to participate and I have – he hasn't.

Iain: How about asking why? How about considering what happens when you do own something difficult for the rest of us to take?

George: Oh, so now you are suggesting that we say, 'Great, well done Hugh. You have totally screwed us up but well done. More power to your elbow.'

Iain: What I am suggesting, George, is that we can learn something from what is going on here and now. What we are doing to each other . . .

Derek: What I have learned is that a chance remark can throw us completely off course.

Paul: Let's get back to the issue of product policy, we need . . .

Iain: Let's not get back to the issue of policy. What is important here is that Hugh has created a major difficulty for us. First we hit him and now we propose to ignore him . . .

Paul: I am not ignoring him. It's not doing us any good poring over the whys and wherefores. Hugh has stated where he stands, all well and good. Now let's get on with it.

Alec: So where do we go?

Iain: Nowhere, unless you face the problem Hugh has given us.

George: No agreed policy, that's what he has given us.

Iain: He has given us an opportunity to examine what we are about. He tells us, clearly, that we have prevented him owning where he was at until now. We may or may not hear that, but we apparently do not like the disruption he is now causing, so we hit him.

Paul: So it's our fault, is it? Our fault that Hugh sits on his hands.

Iain: Not a matter of fault. If we are to develop as a team, we need to be able to explore such issues, however threatening they may appear to be . . .

I will offer one further example before summarizing. You will recall that Eric had substantial problems with regard to what was then termed the strategic decision group which, like a cabinet committee in the United Kingdom parliamentary system, did not

officially exist. Eric, responsible for a substantial part of the
business of the company, was excluded from the deliberations of
this faction of the executive and was most unhappy:

Alec: Look, you don't have to worry about it, Eric. We have
        taken your market into account.
Eric: Where? I can't see it. Either it's in or not. It makes a big
        difference to us as a whole. I know no one but me is
        interested in the non-glamorous end of the business, but
        we get our bread and butter from it, you know. It can't
        simply be ignored.

   In the reorganization which Paul effected subsequent to the
feedback session outlined at the beginning of this chapter, both
Eric and Tony Gent were excluded from the deliberations of the
executive group; they were present only when invited. Paul had
decided to set up a small group to consider strategic issues, to take
decisions regarding the overall shape and direction of the business
and to monitor performance of the various parts of it. Following
precedents in other businesses, he excluded operational managers
from this executive group. His attempt to bring about this system
met substantial resistance from both Eric and Tony, which the
following extracts capture. In the first, Tony and Eric are
discussing their roles with Paul, he has outlined his expectations of
them and they are responding:

Eric: So I am to run my business and someone else is to tell me
        what direction it is to take?
Paul: I didn't say that. I expect you to run your business within
        the overall framework of the company as a whole.
Eric: Which I cannot influence? Have no say in? Like now, only
        worse, I don't get to have any say even after the event.
Tony: It's nonsense, Paul, and you know it. You cannot shut us
        out. You cannot have general managers responding to a
        group. We answer to you, not the executive.
Paul: I am not asking you to answer to the group. You are quite
        right. You answer to me, no doubt about that, and I will
        keep you informed, we can have regular meetings, nothing

will change really, I understand your views . . .

Tony: You are pushing us out, Paul.

Paul: I'm not. That is not my intention. We need to separate tasks, strategy and operations . . .

Eric: Nonsense. Bloody nonsense, Paul, and you know it.

Tony: Total cobblers. Others are pushing you into this. Alec in particular.

Paul: It's not nonsense, Eric. You know how ineffective we have been with all the barons around the table unable to agree anything.

Eric: So we get the push.

Paul: That is not the case. I am very clear that you are key members of my team. You will get all the papers. You are not excluded.

Iain: Just kept out of strategic decision making.

Tony: See. That's it. We are excluded.

Paul: You are not.

Iain: Perhaps you ought to face this, Paul, and be direct. As I understand it, you wish Eric and Tony to play a full part in contributing to strategy formulation in so far and only in so far as it concerns their particular business. They will attend the executive by invitation for these discussions. Otherwise, they will indeed be excluded from that forum.

Paul: Not quite. Eric and Tony are full members of the team, I value them and would want to take their views into account in reaching any decision.

Iain: Understood. But the issue for them here and now is whether or not, as of right, they attend and are full members of the executive and the answer is that they are not.

Paul: They *are* full members. Part of the team. I mean, they will be at *most* meetings . . .

Iain: Why?

Paul: Because of their central role as general managers of key parts of the company.

Iain: So the assumption is that *most* deliberations will be directly concerned with their businesses.

Paul: Not most, but a great deal.

Eric: Why exclude us, then?

Iain: Paul, you are confusing this issue.
Paul: *You* are. Eric and Tony are part of the team.
Iain: Agreed.
Paul: Full stop.
Iain: Not full stop. *Part* of the team but not part of the strategic decision taking group within the company.
Paul: Yes. When what is being discussed affects their business.
Iain: They have no vote. They will be consulted but others will help you decide in their absence.
Eric: That's it. We get to speak, but not to determine action which affects the bottom line of our businesses.
Iain: That's what I take to be the case. You remain part of Paul's team, but are excluded from certain important deliberations.
Tony: Precisely. And that is unacceptable.
Paul: I am not happy with the direction this session is taking.
Iain: What Paul is doing is formalizing what now occurs. You are currently excluded from strategic decision meetings.
Eric: But now he is excluding us from the executive. Not from these meetings but from the executive. That's what I cannot stomach.
Tony: Call it a strategic decision group if you like and I am happy to be out of it.
Iain: As long as you can question its decisions in the executive?
Tony: Yes.
Iain: That has been a mess and that is why, as I understand it, Paul has decided to exclude both you and Eric.
Paul: I don't like the notion of excluding people.

And so on. Enough has been reproduced to give you the flavour of the interaction. In this sequence, as in a number of others, I am pushing for clarity in a circumstance which Paul prefers to maintain ambiguous. My folly is calculated to reveal the essential muddiness of the present and proposed structure by offering a contingency: a structure which, whilst undoubtedly uncomfortable, is less opaque. As it turns out, no one is happy with my attempts. Tony is more concerned with being seen to be excluded from the executive than being excluded from decision making; he is prepared to continue as before, having little influence on strategy but able, as others see it, to 'screw up' subsequent discussion within the executive. Eric's position is less clear, but he does not favour my attempts to have Paul declare where he stands; he wants Paul to include him and sees my attempts to clarify as not conducive to that end. Paul as so often wants the best of both worlds: he wishes to avoid the recriminations which currently absorb time and energy within the executive by excluding Tony and Eric and he wants them to approve of that move. Unable to achieve this, he wishes to soften the edges of his decision and flatter his colleagues into acquiescence. My intervention does not help him in this process.

Matters of authority and fraternity are never resolved once for all and this issue was certainly not settled at this or any subsequent meeting. Whenever Tony or Eric attended executive sessions, they spent considerable amounts of time declaring in one way or another their unhappiness with their status as the exiles: 'I feel like a little boy who is called into the room to say his piece, patted on the head and then sent out straight to bed', or 'I know I have no right to offer an opinion on matters which are the province of my masters, but . . .'

As I indicated earlier, a group such as this is continually engaged in an oscillation between apparently contradictory impulses: the need for authority and the fear of it, the desire to belong and the anxiety of being overwhelmed by others. As consultant to the group, as a fool, it is my role to draw attention to the extremes, to urge the members to experience them and in living through them to learn to handle them. If I can bring about the circumstances where George, Paul and the others struggle to come to terms with the feelings engendered by Hugh's revelation, if I can persuade Paul to be clearer about his anxieties about excluding Eric and Tony, then the next time such a circumstance arises it might be somewhat less difficult to handle. The problem with such an approach, its ultimate folly, is that in seeking to effect this recognition, I am suppressing the very forces that I am seeking to confront. Encouraging George, Paul and the others to deal with the here and now, with the problem that Hugh presents, is inviting them to indulge in the kind of self-disclosure that they fear. Hugh's behaviour in revealing his lack of commitment threatens the group, such revelations may cause it to fly apart, so there is considerable resistance to further disclosure, particularly of the kind I am urging. What is more, exploring the resistance can be seen as even more threatening than the precipitating event. Nonetheless, the enforcement of the exploration process helps the group experience the very ambivalences which have brought about the present circumstance, helps them recognize such 'binds' in the future and helps them find ways of functioning, helps them find a comic mean between elation and despair. A successful piece of folly enables members to learn not only the precise difficulties they have in working together, but also to appreciate the value of trying to come to terms with these difficulties by immersing themselves in them.

Team development, indeed the executive process itself, is an iterative process. Within the group, progress can be measured in terms of the members' ability to recognize and confront the ambivalences which are within the group and to find a way of handling them. The oscillation or iterations provide the experience within which members, in allowing themselves to experience fully the tensions and emotion associated with authority and fraternity, can develop, can learn how to handle these experiences the next time around. Denying the tensions and emotions serves to hold the group in place, for ever marking time, unable to move on. Addressing them threatens the very existence of the team and, paradoxically, simultaneously enables it to truly become a team. To reconcile conflicting instincts and interests, we need to know what they are; to own them fully appears to threaten any possibility of reconciliation. There are only two ways forward: an act of faith, in which we all join, or an act of folly, in which individuals are forced to confront that which they so assiduously maintain is not there.

There remains the possibility that the fool has it wrong: that my view of the circumstances and my imposition of that view upon others is fundamentally misguided. It is, of course, a matter of interpretation.[1]

The notion of interpreting a playscript is readily accepted in the theatre; one cannot just 'do' a play, the text is not neutral. There are several ways of 'doing' *Hamlet*; no one of them is authoritative, each is an act of interpretation, of making a 'reading' and projecting that reading so that we as audience may also be guided in our understanding of what *Hamlet* is about.

Performance involves selection and choice: of setting, of costumes, of actors, of rhythm, of colour, of pitch, emphasis and pace. Such choices must be made on what appear to be relevant grounds and the consideration of such grounds is a matter of interpretation. There is simply no way of creating in advance, as it were, a full 'score' for *Hamlet* (or any other play); such a score would have to specify moment by moment 'sizes, shapes, colours, inflections, tones of voice, word emphasis, rhythms, duration of pauses, placements of actors on stage, movement, tempos and so on and would require thousands of pages and would still be less precise than the score of Beethoven's Fifth Symphony'.[2] When we witness a performance we witness an event around which someone, somewhere has made a series of choices as to its meaning. To simply 'do' a play without making choices as to interpretation is not possible. Nor is it possible to present the product of research into interaction without exercising some choices; data does not speak for itself. In selecting, shaping and presenting the material each of us exercises choice; we commit to paper an interpretation of what we have witnessed, the better to guide our readers. In beginning this book as I have done I have performed an aesthetic function. Out of several score pages of transcript I have selected and edited four or five. I have not presented you with all of the coughs, sighs, grunts, false starts and the like that were a feature of the 'real' interaction.[3] My very choice of this particular passage is the result of an interpretation; segmentation of the text is relative to a particular interpretation. When I as a commentator, at the lowest level of redescription, identify a passage as a segment by assigning to it an interpretative description, the nature and form of the segment is determined by a choice of description somewhat higher up in the interpretative hierarchy. Until such a choice is made, there is no basis for the identification of the passage as a segment. Clearly, if it is the case that any one interpretation creates or determines the material it explains, then it becomes self-confirming: 'The same text can sponsor quite different data (though some of the data will remain constant), and each set of data will very powerfully support the interpretative theory which sponsored it in the first place.'[4] Interpretation is inevitable and a matter of consequence. Some choices, however, are better than others and it is to these rules of interpretation that I now turn.

There are four criteria which can normally be used to judge interpretations: completeness, correctness, comprehensiveness and consistency.[5] Completeness and correctness are based upon the requirement for all description ('scientific' or otherwise): plausibility. Comprehensiveness and consistency are of a different order; one can challenge an interpretation as being incomplete or incorrect (in the manner in which I will use the terms) without necessarily having another interpretation in mind, but one can only challenge on grounds of comprehensiveness and consistency when one has an alternative. Such challenges are mounted in the name of acceptability. The distinction will become clearer below.

Completeness of interpretation of a particular sequence (such as that involving George and Paul) may be said to occur when it has been considered in terms of subject, status, tone and style. An interpretative description of a segment or sequence may be said to be complete if it deals with the contribution each of these aspects makes to a higher level description. The description of the subject is the core around which the description of the tone, the status and the style can be woven. But one must not ignore other aspects. What occurs in the sequence with which we are concerned involves more than the two principal speakers. To be sure the tone of George is one of extravagant self-flagellation and that of Paul one of increasing asperity, but that is not all there is to be said about the tone: there is an overall tone which is produced by the interaction between the tones of George and Paul and by a further aspect of what occurs. Or to be correct, what does not occur. No one else speaks but each by posture or gesture comments upon the exchanges, Derek finally summing it all up in 'Anyone for coffee?' In effect the tone of the interaction is set more by these responses than by anything the principal speakers say.

In a similar fashion one can determine the subject of the sequence by reference to the reactions of the others present in the scene. Indeed I offer such an interpretation: they have seen it all before, 'it' being the playing out of the relationship between George and Paul. As I have indicated, the subject is the core of an interpretation and as such is the area which offers the widest scope for disagreement. Some may hold, for example, that the subject of the passage is the loss the company is making and that the tone with which we should be concerned is the attitude towards that loss displayed by George and Paul. To reject such a conclusion I would need to go beyond the particular speeches made by George and Paul and consider the reaction to them on the part of everyone else. The speeches have a status within the passage as a whole which is determined by the reactions to them. Assume, for the sake of argument, that everyone had fallen about in hysterical laughter once George and Paul set to; how would we have then interpreted the speeches? Or assume that each member had responded to George and joined in to defend himself from charges of dereliction of duty – what then would we make of the sequence?

Failure to take explicit notice of the status of a passage may lead the interpreter to ignore the important question about its significance relative to an overall theme. To appreciate the significance of the 'To be or not to be' lines in *Hamlet*, the playgoer must know that they are spoken by a Hamlet suffering from dreadful revelations put forward concerning his mother and his uncle. The speech is not a direct statement of the theme of the play. In a similar fashion, George's outburst about the company loss is not a direct statement about the nature of executive interaction in this particular company. In the context of similar outbursts by George concerning different issues and similar responses from Paul, one can see this particular exchange as part of some larger theme.

In any event the passage, like all others involving these particular improvisators, has an identifiable style. George and his colleagues use a certain vocabulary, a certain syntax, a certain punctuation, a certain range of rhetorical devices; contrast, exaggeration, rhythm, certain types of image. George's speeches are embellished with rhetorical exclamations every few lines, for example, and form a pattern with the calmer, initially more measured tones of Paul.

A description of subject, tone, status and style, although it may hang together, can be challenged as incorrect. I may hold that the passage is yet one more expression of the ability of this particular group to ignore each other. I make this interpretation in the context of having witnessed many other scenes like this one and support it by reference to the behaviour of all others in the room save George and Paul. I sustain it by reference to tone, status and style; in other words my interpretation is complete. Nonetheless, it may be challenged as incorrect given that George and Paul appear to be a long way from being disengaged.

To challenge a particular interpretation one does not need an alternative, but one does need to be able to show that the interpretation being advanced either is simply incorrect (the tone of the passage overall is one of anger not acceptance or resignation) or is incomplete – it does not adequately cover the points at issue. 'What about this? How can this be covered by your interpretation?' To be sure, in mounting a challenge one may wish to substitute another interpretation, but the plausibility of a particular perspective does not depend upon there being a better one to hand.

The explanatory power of an interpretation depends upon its ability to interrelate sequences such as the one with which I am concerned into a pattern. A particular analysis may be plausible (complete and correct), but it also needs to be acceptable (complete, correct, comprehensive and consistent). Assume that my interpretation of this sequence is that it demonstrates the ability of the group as a whole not to be drawn into angry exchanges but to be able to ignore disagreements, as George and Paul eventually appear to do. Does it accord with other sequences I have observed with this group? Are there occasions where it does not? Is the interpretation comprehensive? Or is there a better one that subsumes activities at a higher level of description?

Assume that we have another extract to consider from behaviour in the Boardroom where George does in fact behave in front of the directors precisely as instructed not to by Paul. He goes in and puts on a similar performance to that which has been reproduced above. It would, perhaps, still be possible to interpret the exchanges as a whole as having to do with the relations between George and Paul, but it would be difficult to hang on to the overall view of the interactions as a sequence where some minimal commitment to workable relations is the *raison d'être* of the group. George's actions would force us to reconsider the events as either tragic or melodramatic depending upon the nature of this hypothetical scene; a comprehensive analysis would have to encompass both the scene with which I began this book and all others.

Where an interpretation cannot be extended we can talk of 'resistance'. Resistance is a relative quality; any passage is resistant in different degrees to different interpretations. It follows that one interpretation is more comprehensive than another if it leaves a smaller and less significant part of the scene resistant to

interpretation. Comprehensiveness is a criterion for the acceptability of an interpretation because of the principle of functionality,
i.e. the convention that all of the identifiable aspects of an
exchange should be sociologically relevant, which I take to be part
of the institution of social science itself. Ideally any series of scenes
or segments may be taken to be potentially significant and analysed
so that no part is resistant to interpretation. An interpretation is
more comprehensive than another interpretation if it leaves a
smaller part of the material resistant to interpretation.

I cannot arrive at a comprehensive interpretation if passages
within the text as a whole are inconsistent. In the hypothetical
scene of George performing in front of the external directors just
as he does in front of his colleagues we have a sequence
-depending upon the reactions of the other actors – which may not
be consistent with any other sequences we have observed. Whether
or not this is a major inconsistency in seeking to interpret the
activities of this group as stuck is a matter for judgement; what is
clear is that an interpretation is more consistent than another if it
leaves fewer and less important groups of elements resistant to
interpretation. If an exhaustive analysis is possible and all the
scenes and acts (groups of scenes) can be integrated into one
interpretation, then we can talk of the activities of this particular
team having coherence. The quality is desirable because as social
scientists (perhaps as Western educated human beings) we have a
theory of value which says that which manifests coherence is
preferable to that which displays incoherence.

Given this approach to the analysis of qualitative data one can
offer interpretations or readings of sequences such as that
occurring between George and his colleagues which are more or
less plausible, more or less acceptable. One can deal in detail with
particular scenes and one can deal with an entire script or drama –
the drama of executive action.

It is my contention that the most effective and useful role the
consultant can play is that of the fool; without folly, without the
kind of metatheatrical perspective he or she provides, there is
unlikely to be an opportunity for reflection or learning. Nonetheless, many of us go beyond this function and seek fame, fortune
and immortality by attempting to help members of the organization
rewrite their scripts. Some of us even become involved in coaching

and direction, acting as both audience and critic to those we have so carefully groomed for stardom.

At Friction Free Castings, as elsewhere, I offered my services as dramaturge and became heavily involved in the redesign of the organization, the definition and allocation of roles and the writing and rewriting of scripts specific to the revised circumstances. I was particularly enthusiastic about a process we termed 'ratting' (Role Analysis Technique), whereby each one of the senior managers determined his role in association with his colleagues and each team in the organization agreed its role. These sessions were marked by an attempt upon my part and that of the members to confront problems and resolve them.

An example will illustrate the principles involved. Below is an early attempt to define the role of the new executive team at Friction Free Castings.

Role of the Friction Free Executive as a Team

1   To develop the Company strategy.
2   To ensure that the strategy is implemented.
3   To define and agree operational objectives.
4   To monitor performance against strategic and operational objectives.
5   To take decisions on operations across more than one Business.
6   To agree financial objectives for each Business or Company and to advise on what is needed to achieve them.
7   To be accountable for the overall financial results.
8   To agree and commit to the overall forecast.
9   To ensure that product cost targets of the overall strategy are met.
10   To approve plans.
11   To provide support, guidance and help in preparation of plans.
12   To review regularly major Company-wide projects.
13   To take decisions on major organizational changes.
14   To approve the borrowing limits for each Business and for the Company.
15   To approve the disbursement of Company assets.

Summary of Executive Role

(a) The principal role of the executive team is to bring about change in the Company. In this role, the central functions must provide support, where this is required by a general manager, to help him implement his objectives.

(b) The second fundamental role is to provide strong central direction.

These aspirations have, of course, to be tested against at least two other sets of aspirations, those of the Managing Director and those of the general managers. The latter took themselves to be responsible to Paul, the Managing Director, for some aspects of this list and were most unhappy with statements such as 'To take decisions on operations across more than one business', and 'To monitor performance against strategic and operational objectives'. Needless to say, a considerable amount of anxiety over matters of authority and fraternity was generated by this exercise and it took several sessions before a sufficient measure of agreement was reached to enable the group to begin to function with confidence that its remit ran wider than the executive suite. Even some months after these initial attempts to clarify parts to be played and the manner in which they were to be enacted, exchanges such as the following were not uncommon:

Eric: The issue has not gone away, Paul. I am excluded from decisions which affect my business and people who have no knowledge of it decide for me what I am to do.

Paul: That's not fair, Eric, and you know it. You are called in whenever there is a discussion about Parts and Service.

Eric: True. When it is specifically labelled P and S I am there, but P and S is involved in every aspect of the business. Licensing in Norway, that's got implications for us, but I wasn't asked.

Other comments and disagreements were matters of authority:

Tony: I work for you, as I understand it, and I expect you to monitor me directly. Not through Alec or George or anyone else, for that matter.

Paul: Correct, you work for me.

Tony: And only you. The others are colleagues at the same level as me, I take it. Advisers to you if you choose to listen to them, but with no authority over me or mine . . .

This kind of interaction was matched on the other side by exchanges within the executive of a similar nature, but coming to the opposite conclusion:

Alec: We have to be clear about who is responsible for what. If we – as a team – are responsible for the bottom line, Tony and Eric have to follow our directions.

Paul: In principle, yes . . .

George: What do you mean, in principle . . .? Either they do or they do not.

Paul: Through me they are responsible. We decide here and I tell them.

Alec: Who monitors compliance?

Paul: We do. I do . . . I and you to keep me informed.

Alec: But you do not have the time. We cannot be running back and forth to you every time something crops up. 'Paul, will you please tell Eric to do this or that.'

I could go on and provide further examples [6] of interactions occurring both within and outside the executive team, but all would highlight the continuing struggle around authority and fraternity. Throughout, my role remained the same: it was to draw attention to these referents and to seek to have those directly involved in improvising around them live with the extremes, move towards a comic mean epitomizing neither denial nor melodramatic assault. My position was, and is, that authority and fraternity will always be matters of concern to senior executives and that movement, escape from debilitating routines, will only occur when extreme positions are explored. Members need to experience fully the anxiety about being directed and having no direction, about being overwhelmed by the group and having no commitment to it; all four extremes are part of the team's world and immersion in each of the conditions is the ultimate paradox by which the members can move. If, as Paul's team was, a group is transfixed with anxiety about one or other position, it cannot and will not move; fearing the worst, it can never discover that which may be better; hoping for the best, it cannot tolerate something less good than it currently experiences. The effectiveness of teams such as Paul's depends upon the ability to display conflicting instincts and interests, to celebrate them in their full diversity, to experience the dissonance and, having done that, to reconcile them. If the team is unable to immerse itself in conflict, to experience counterdependence, it cannot fully move towards a middle ground; if, on the other hand, it does not immerse itself in 'group think', it cannot experience dependence. Experiencing neither pole, no subsequent comic middle ground can be reached. The team needs to recognize that it lives in a world in which extremes exist and must be owned. The comic stance implies a *measured* acceptance of the world, in all its fundamental disparateness – not, repeat not, an avoidance of position, not an easy acceptance that anything is OK, but a balance of contrarieties.

Paul's group, like many executive groups, sought a mid position without allowing itself to explore the range. Even after reflection, members sought to deny the intensity of oppositional forces. Hugh was attacked for revealing that he felt under pressure to conform, and Paul, as I have shown, sought to deny that he was excluding Tony and Eric from the major part of deliberations within the team whilst also denying the authority of those within the team. I will conclude once more with my assertion that the function of an executive group is 'to facilitate the synthesis in concrete action of contradictory forces, to reconcile conflicting forces, instincts, interests, conditions, positions and ideals'. Taking away or denying the opportunity for expressing and exploring these forces, these instincts, interests, conditions, positions and ideals results in a group that experiences the tensions and emotions but has no way of handling them. The more denial such groups manifest, the more attempts they make to reduce anxiety, to 'move on and get the job done', the more the pressure mounts to express conflicting positions. To have any chance of movement, individuals and teams must be given opportunity to experience and explore that which they find most challenging, that which is at the centre of their anxieties: matters of authority and fraternity.

6 Checking at Feathers

Interventions such as mine, that focus directly upon the quality of relationships among members of a team and seek to discuss that which hitherto has been taken to be beyond the pale, often succeed in changing member attitudes and sometimes affect actual behaviour in groups.[1] Paul's team was not an exception to this rule.

Before the intervention, Paul's group had little or no sense of direction; members either lacked objectives or had ones which conflicted; priorities changed weekly and were not monitored; members were engaged by their work, they clearly cared about what they were doing and for the future of the company, but poor work was tolerated and good work went unrewarded. After the intervention, there was a sense of direction, there were clear shared objectives and, for a time, an attempt to monitor them. Mediocre performance, however, continued not to be distinguished from that which was good or excellent.

Before the intervention, everyone had to 'fight his own corner' and no one spoke for the overall company perspective. Conflicts simmered away under the surface and occasionally erupted, at which point no one dealt with them creatively or constructively. Despite attempts by a small faction of the executive, planning was accorded a low priority and strategy was regarded as an unwarranted invasion of territory. After the intervention, excessive advocacy of particular business perspectives was regarded as unacceptable, the company perspective became paramount; differences in views, moreover, were regarded as important matters to be surfaced and expressed in order to arrive at strategy which became the dominant concern of most members.

Before the intervention, coaching was neglected; Paul had not been known to provide personal advice to any of his managers. Process advice was unheard of and no one within the group or external to it ever offered a comment upon its operations. After the intervention, I spent a considerable amount of individual time with Paul and each member of his team, as well as with the team as a whole, counselling and advising them about matters of style, relationships and decision process. A number of them developed and deployed their skills of intervention to good effect within the team.

A considerable amount of movement was, therefore, discernible within the activities of the executive; they were, on the report of themselves and of others, less stuck in their routines. They showed respect for and interest in differing opinions and, on a number of occasions, encouraged the expression and exploration of conflicts. For a time, perhaps a year or so, the team enjoyed a productive period. Participation and trust were at a higher level in the group than any of the members had previously experienced and than I had experienced in this team or any other. Difficulties were surfaced and confronted, not without confusion and anxiety and not always with acceptable outcomes but, nonetheless, no one flinched, initially, from facing them. Gradually, however, almost imperceptibly, the group slipped back into its old ways of handling circumstances. In particular, the reaction of the members to Paul took on a less than confronting form despite – or perhaps even because of – his repeated request for feedback about his own performance. The problem as seen by the members was that when Paul was confronted about particular issues, he appeared contrite, even apologetic, and resolved to remedy matters but then signally failed to do so.

The matter of who was involved in decision making about strategy and, later, operations dogged the group for months. Paul had accepted the notion that the executive was to contribute to the making of decisions, but, in practice, it was widely perceived that whatever he may have agreed in the Boardroom he failed to implement once he left it. On several occasions, the team, with the full participation of Paul and with a considerable degree of skill, came to conclusions which resulted in little or no action: messages began to filter back about the ineffectiveness of the group and relations within the team became strained once more.

The leader's function in a team such as that at Friction Free Castings is clear.[2] He is there to monitor the performance of the team and individual members of it and to take whatever action is necessary to resolve difficulties as they arise. In a circumstance where the team is charged with the reconciliation of difficulties, his role in keeping them to that task is crucial. The team's failure is, in the final analysis, Paul's failure. As before, he became part of the problem, and his vacillation and indecision sapped their energy and enthusiasm.

It would be tempting to end on such a note, to claim that, but for Paul, the intervention would have been a success. Tempting, but not reasonable. The renewed attacks and the failure to implement agreed decisions could be construed as a resurfacing of earlier problems, classic matters of authority and fraternity which my foolishness had failed to resolve. There can be no doubt that as time went by I became less and less useful to the group. I became an officially appointed court jester, no longer on the fringes of respectability and less and less marginal as the days went by.[3] I assumed a substantially remunerated and duly acknowledged position of considerable influence. I helped Paul redesign the organization, I helped him select his team, I produced and ran the 'ratting' process, I had the ears of most of the senior managers inside and outside the team.

As I behaved more as an adviser, I became more predictable. Rather than standing aside from matters of authority and fraternity, I too began to structure my own behaviour around these referents: I wished to be influential and was happy to belong. The more I moved from the periphery of the organization to its centre, the more my folly lost its vitality.

Even had I played my part better than I did, there could have been no guarantee that my intervention would have been successful. The idea of intervention, coming between, rendering the familiar strange, relies upon the creation of distance between an actor and his part, between the espoused theory and the theory in action. Such a theory seems to take no account of the fact that distance tends to close rapidly. Everything, everywhere, seeks its own illusory level and foolishness is no exception to the rule. Foolishness, which in my terms serves to infiltrate a question between actor and action, all too soon is assimilated by those exposed to it. Just as in the theatre I become accustomed to the artificial sets and even to Brecht's exposure of their very artificiality, so in social life I can render conventional almost any attempt to alienate me from what I do. Some degree of impudence was expected of me and, over time, was accepted, tolerated and discounted. I lost my power to shock and with it went whatever real influence I may have had.

One of the consequences of my intervention and my subsequent lack of marginality was that Paul's role became, over time, less democratic and more absolute. As he concentrated authority into his own hands, particularly arrogated to himself the power to implement decisions, he became cut off from those who ought to have been closest to him. He could not afford to confide in his executive since, as important actors in the decision making process, they could expect and demand influence in the process of implementing decisions and he could not confide in his general managers since they would expect and demand influence upon the decision making process. I did not represent a threat to him on either score (although I should have done so on both) and could become a confidant. Owing to my perceived marginality, I was embraced as a potential listener and intimate, but that very initial marginality was compromised by the confidences. I was debarred from putting to political use the knowledge which I derived through these exchanges since, outside of this dyad, the knowledge was confidential. Inside it, I could listen, counsel and advise but, over the months, our thoughts became as one; we both became estranged from the rest of the organization, each a mirror-image to the other, sustained in the illusion that we were having an effect.

The absolute ruler, unchallenged in his absolutism, is isolated and this has, and had, consequences. Paul lacked information. Here again, as with the court fool of old, I filled the structural void. It has been noted that the court jesters 'roamed through the court and through the city in order to gather information for their monarch which they reported back to him upon their return'.[4] On a number of occasions, I played a similar role for Paul, providing him with both gossip and solid information about aspects of his policy and his decision making. To be sure, this was done in order to cause him to explicitly address the issues that had prompted the stories, but where nothing was done (and action as a consequence of the information became less and less frequent), my services simply served to reinforce his isolation. Members of his executive and others sought to channel information through me such that gradually I began to function as a kind of passage to the summit of power.[5]

The more isolated and absolutist Paul became, the more I functioned as a buffer between him and the rest of his senior managers. As I have shown, initially I challenged Paul in the group and privately and was able 'to get away with it'; indeed, he encouraged me to do so and appeared to pay attention to what I had to say. These challenges became less and less frequent as time passed and, like much of my behaviour, became predictable and licensed. Indeed, by allowing me the kind of impudence I demonstrated, by encouraging me to raise problems with him directly, Paul and I between us showed everyone else how inconsequential they actually were.

> Precisely because the fool was allowed to ridicule the king and because he was even at times allowed to mount the throne and sway his 'marotte' – that sceptre of parasitical power – the monarch demonstrated to all present the true nature of his sovereignty. The humiliation of everyone with political aspirations must have been complete![6]

As in the medieval court, so in Friction Free Castings. Paul's absolutist tendencies were heightened by a circumstance in which only I – the officially appointed fool – could challenge him and that challenge itself became more feeble as the days passed.

In a sense, I have become a victim of my own analogy. A court fool had to know the tastes and ideas of his master. He had to be able to read his mind swiftly, he had to know when the king favoured and when he disliked. When a change occurred, the fool had to register it and adjust on the hoof, as it were:

> He must observe their mood on whom he jests,
> The quality of persons, and the time;
> And, like the haggard, check at every feather
> That comes before his eye. This is a practice
> As full of labour as a wise man's art;
> For folly that he wisely shows is fit;
> But wise men, folly-fall'n, quite taint their wit.[7]

As Paul became less and less inclined to implement decisions that he had encouraged his team to discuss and conclude, as he took less and less notice of my folly, I became cautious. I observed his mood, took account of the company that he kept (and remained silent on many occasions) and, in particular, I became obsessed with matters of timing. I convinced myself that there was a time and a place to intervene for maximum effect and it was rarely now. I attempted wise folly, I tried to make my comments fit the temper of the times and, in so doing, remained in employment but had a diminishing impact upon Paul or his team. In a sense I became a diversion rather than a force, an entertainer rather than a disturbance. Caution did not pay off; in art and life, one has to go too far before one can learn how far is far enough.

Like many an intervention, mine succeeded in changing attitudes and behaviour in the group for a time, but it had no lasting or consistent impact on group performance. Indeed it could be said to be counterproductive since it brought about the temporary dismantling of defences and raised expectations in a manner which was seen as costly to the individuals involved. Quite a number of Paul's colleagues expressed regret that their open comments to me, given at some perceived risk, had not resulted in long term substantial change.

What does this imply beyond my own incompetence and the inability of Paul to trust his colleagues? Not surprisingly, events at Friction Free Castings simply serve to reinforce our knowledge of the complexities of behaviour in organizations and the problems of effecting change. Much of the literature on the dynamics of behaviour in organizations and virtually all of it concerned with the management of change is simplistic and, in many instances, based more upon wishful thinking than observation, description, analysis or theory. The term 'organization' implies more orderliness, coordination and systematic behaviour than is evident to most of us who operate within such institutions, and the commonly promoted definition of organizational change assumes an entity that is, a possibility that could be, and a plan that realizes the possibility. If, as I have implied, disorder is the normal condition rendered less chaotic by the imposition of scripts upon it, then it follows that change, not order, is the norm. Managers work hard to make sense of that which surrounds them, particularly the actions and interactions of other managers. Scripts help to create order but must be frequently enacted to check that the routines still work and everyone is sticking to his or her part. Order is produced, sustained, challenged and reconstituted through the enactment of everyday interactions, patterns of mindless behaviour which nonetheless collapse without warning. 'Business as usual' is no empty cliché – it is an achievement against the odds as individuals, pairs and groups daily create and re-create their environment.

My position, outlined earlier, is that much of what occurs is appropriately mindless but that each and every aspect of 'organization' is vulnerable simply because in the final analysis it is based upon face-to-face interaction. Goffman captures the essence of what I am trying to say:

> A great deal of the work of organizations – decision making, the transmission of information, the close coordination of physical tasks – is done face to face, requires being done in this way, and is vulnerable to face-to-face effects. Differently put, in so far as agents of social organizations of any scale from states to households, can be persuaded, cajoled, flattered, intimidated, or otherwise influenced by effects only achievable in face-to-face dealings, then here, too, the interactive order blatantly impinges on macroscopic entities.[8]

The role of top management is to prevent disintegration, to reduce the incidence of discretion implicit in face-to-face interaction and to render mindless as much behaviour as possible. The dilemma it faces in so doing is that it is all too successful and not only creates alienation around itself but succumbs to the condition itself. In the urge to reduce ambiguity, to contain fragmentation, to establish participation and to delineate authority, the very attributes that may be vital to the survival of the enterprise are squeezed out. I have argued that diversity of opinion, dissent and open conflict are necessary to the development of a genuine consensus (without which all *planned* action will fail). Unfortunately, in many senior teams, the fear is that expressions of dissent and conflict engender fragmentation and dissolution of the team itself which exists to contain or reconcile these very conflicts. What is more, even talking about the possibility of such conflicts, tied as such discussion would seem to be to matters of authority and fraternity, is itself a circumstance to be avoided. There are a number of paradoxes involved in all of this: top teams must promote mindless behaviour if the enterprise is to achieve any sense of direction and feeling of cohesion but success will render the enterprise unresponsive to its environment; top teams must reconcile conflicts of interests but cannot do so without identifying them and in so doing risk their own cohesiveness; a new consensus can only be achieved by destroying the old one; revised beliefs upon which actions are to be founded can only arise from that which was previously determined to be correct; the only way to break free of ideas that preserve cohesion, continuity and the old consensus is to render them vulnerable but such attempts will be resisted simply because they may achieve the desired condition.

At Friction Free Castings, I was able to create the circumstances where the improvisation around authority and fraternity were challenged. There were occasions in which fundamental differences of opinion were surfaced, examined, discussed and productively reconciled. There were, of course, other occasions upon which I and the other members of the team were less successful. The problem, however, lay not in the impossibility of the task. Here, as in other organizations, it was possible to create conditions in which challenge was acceptable and ambiguity the subject of greater tolerance; the problem was to sustain these conditions for long.

It can be done providing that matters of authority, fraternity and emotion are constantly to the forefront of all concerned. My very success in having members of Paul's team address issues of authority and fraternity caused me to lose focus at the point of seeking to institutionalize those perspectives. I failed on two counts, both important. The first was to fail to pay proper attention to the excluded: to Tony and Eric. They ceased to be members of Paul's immediate team and, as exiles, found their position very difficult to bear. As I have shown, a number of attempts were made to confront the issues of both exclusion and authority, but none was successful and I did not maintain my effort to resolve these matters. In retrospect, it is clear that upsetting both authority and fraternity in this manner made their positions and that of both the team and Paul towards them intolerably ambiguous. In such circumstances, Tony and Eric sought reassurance from Paul who was more than happy to give it but could only maintain the position he thus put himself in by keeping the team and the dissenting duo away from each other. In effect, he did a deal with Tony and Eric – 'you really are part of my team' – whilst maintaining to George and the others that this was not the case. Needless to say, this satisfied no one; Tony and Eric sought to demonstrate that they were involved as full members and the others sought to totally exclude them from anything but narrowly defined operational matters. The lack of resolution of a fundamental issue is clear in the following extract when Tony and Eric are talking with Paul about their own role as general managers. Paul has excluded the executive from this discussion:

Tony: And we report directly to you?
Paul: Yes.
Tony: On every matter?
Paul: I don't see what you are driving at. Yes.
Eric: So on matters of product development, personnel, finance, manufacturing, marketing and so on, it's you and us.
Paul: Except in so far as it's strategy, then it's the executive.
Tony: But you said we have only one boss. You.
Paul: Yes. You report to me but I expect you to work with Alec on strategy, Hugh on products . . .
Eric: That's it, you see. Either I run my business, responsible to you, as they do, or not. There cannot be a half-way house.
Paul: They report to me as well and I am looking for cooperation.
Eric: But there is only one bottom line and it's mine – yours, really, but you hold me accountable. Not Alec, not George – me.
Paul: You have only one boss – me.

At another time in another arena – that of the executive team – Paul elaborates another version of events:

Alec: So on matters of strategy elaboration, I can go straight to Tony.

Paul: I don't see why not.
Alec: And Tony's men?
Paul: Well, that's different. Through him, I would suggest.
Alec: But we all know what his response is likely to be. Two
         fingers. 'This is my business – keep out.'
Paul: That's not likely to be the case. I will talk to him.
Alec: And monitoring the performance. After we set the
         strategy, who is to monitor it?
George: We must, of course. At a company level, we monitor
         achievement.
Alec: Paul?
Paul: Yes. It comes here. We look at it and decide what needs
         to be done.

The problems are evident to anyone with the most rudimentary
of perceptions. I certainly did not miss the issues and sought to
address them, but my main focus was upon the executive, not upon
the relations between it and the rest of the organization. Paul
placed himself between the group and the rest of the organization
and became the interpreter of events, the provider of meanings in a
manner which served to rekindle all the old suspicions. And I
allowed him to do it. In seeking to implement and sustain a
particular course of action, one must recognize that those
displaced by it will seek to reverse their positions and one must not
underestimate their capability of doing just that; the dynamics of
authority and fraternity become even more intense as an old order
is shaken and a new one emerges.

I have mentioned my own flirtation with authority and fraternity.
It was not a casual affair, nor was it without encouragement from
my colleagues. Alec, George and the others smoothed the way,
stimulated Paul to talk to me, threw us together, acted as pimps for
the inevitable liaison, flattered me with their earnest pleas: 'He will
listen to you. You had better speak to him about it. He will take it
more from you.' Not that the result can be laid entirely at their
door. I was attracted by the heady perfume of authority, perhaps
there was a short cut to resolving matters of authority, a word from
me and Paul would understand. Matters of authority and fraternity
can only be resolved by those directly involved in them, they cannot
be dealt with by sending messengers, particularly when the

messenger himself is susceptible to the blandishments of authority: 'Between us, we can sort this one out, Iain.'

Finally, in this catalogue of errors, I underestimated the problem of individual emotion. Matters of authority and fraternity are always accompanied by emotion, and changes in such aspects of relationships inevitably produce strong reactions. Indeed, as I have stated earlier, many emotions may be said to arise from actual or imagined threats to authority and fraternity. It is one thing to 'know' this intellectually, quite another to pay atention to it in seeking to handle change. Individuals such as George, Alec, Tony and Eric may generate very high levels of anxiety not only as they confront matters of authority and fraternity, but also as they fail to confront them. High levels of emotion accompanied as they are by psychological disturbance (palpitations, breathlessness, headache or whatever) make it extremely difficult for individuals to hear things, to process information, to focus or pay attention. The members of Friction Free Castings were subject to considerable stress throughout this intervention and, not surprisingly, varied in their ability to cope with it. One or two physically withdrew from potentially anxiety-inducing sessions by absenting themselves from work, some withdrew within sessions by gazing out of the window, some sought to render the events more predictable by demanding or proposing elaborate, structured agendas, some simply resorted to uproar techniques – 'Look, it's getting late, we are getting nowhere, wasting time and money, let's pack it in and get back to some real work.' Paul suffered more than most, since he elected to bear the brunt of the 'blame' for the present circumstances and he placed himself in the ambivalent position of interpreter of the group to those who had been excluded. The psychic cost to him was large, manifest in his drained appearance, his inability to sleep well and his irresolution once away from the group.

The implications for the management of change from the preceding discussion are, I think, relatively straightforward. First, if, as I have argued, authority and fraternity are key factors in both the executive process and the movement towards the establishment of such a process, then care must be taken to identify those involved in the transition and to square them. If they cannot be squared, if they find it impossible to reconcile themselves to a shift, then they must be removed. In the present case, Tony and Eric were unlikely to accept an effective demotion from the top team and were then unlikely to cooperate in new patterns of authority. They completely rejected the new model, even in the fudged version put to them by Paul, and as key players in the organization, they were able to subvert it. This very issue should have been the subject of a conversation with them rather than a matter to be avoided or smoothed over with talk of their 'really' being a part of the team. In effecting any change, care must be taken to address and thereafter manage the key actors. Some will be for the change, some neutral and some against. The last consist of those who are likely to be disfranchised by it. If, as is most probable, they cannot be brought to support it, they must not remain in a position to undermine it.

Second, and equally important, the leader has a powerful influence upon the way events develop. Paul's courage in facing up to the problems of his organization was of the highest order; he could have taken the report and shelved it, he could have emasculated it or used it vindictively.[9] He did none of these, choosing rather to own the material and to explore its implications with his colleagues. For a while, he behaved admirably as a leader, seeking through his own behaviour and through his explicit statements to move his team towards the vision of the executive process that he had elaborated in early conversations with me. On a number of occasions, his example was crucial in encouraging his team to surface, discuss and reconcile matters of considerable pain and anguish. Leaders send important signals through the organization, the more so during times of high uncertainty such as created in a transition period. They are looked to for indications as to meaning and directions for appropriate behaviour; even the most trivial actions are studied for indications of desired behaviour. The leader's role at moments of transition is to articulate the vision (in association with his colleagues), to use the reward system to promote it and his formal power where necessary to remove unreasonable opposition to it. Despite the heavy emphasis placed in these pages upon the essentially democratic nature of the executive process, there remains a clear and unambiguous role for the formal leader. It is his or her role to legitimate the particular structure of relations which arises to support the vision. All systems of control must grapple with issues of diversity, uncertainty, scarcity, direction and the like. By validating a particular grouping to do this, other players are ruled out, a hierarchy, willy-nilly, is created. There is nothing to be gained by pretending this is not the case.

Some leaders, and Paul was probably one such, are more transactional than charismatic.[10] Transactional leaders manipulate rewards and punishments, whereas charismatic leaders transcend such means and actively inculcate new meanings in their followers. Burns notes that such behaviour 'becomes moral in that it raises the level of human conduct and ethical aspiration of both the leader and the led, and this has a transforming effect on both'.[11] Transactional leaders sustain patterns of organization and relationships which help to support a particular distribution of power. This is not to claim that transactional leaders do not promote adaptation; where routines are inadequate, they promote – through rewards and punishments – more appropriate responses. Where, as in the present case, participants begin to question the very nature of authority, the underlying values of the organization, transactional relations may not be sufficient to hold the enterprise together. Under such circumstances (those that obtain at any time of substantial change), explicit ideological formulations, mutually developed or leader articulated, may be required to justify new patterns of behaviour. Even here it is probably worth distinguishing between catalytic leadership and charismatic leadership. Highly emotional and personally involved outpourings of energy appear to be part of both kinds of leadership. In the catalytic form, however, the leader does not introduce new meanings to followers, rather he or she surfaces and articulates that which already exists. In the charismatic relationship, leaders do not simply catalyse change to make manifest what was latent, they actually create and 'sell' new ideas.

The glimmerings of a continuum of leadership may be discerned in all of this. A charismatic leader may be needed to convince those of us lacking vision that an executive team based upon a thoroughly open, confronting yet supportive and reconciling style is possible; a catalytic leader is needed to operate such a style (surfacing and articulating the attitudes of all concerned); and a transactional leader is needed to institutionalize and sustain the pattern. Each aspect of leadership is important but, at moments of

transition, without the charismatic, without the ability to restruc-
ture the world and endow it with legitimacy, little will change.
Transformations involving the destruction of old patterns and the
improvisation of new responses, particularly where matters of
authority and fraternity are involved, constitute the most demanding tasks of a leader. He or she must generate or be persuaded of
the efficacy and desirability of new meanings, and then they must
effect this transformation amongst their colleagues and followers.
Success at this first stage does not guarantee success at later stages.

Paul was never completely convinced of the new order, even
though some of his colleagues were. Accordingly, even had he
been capable of it, he never fully articulated the vision or sold it
throughout his organization. He continued to behave as a
transactional leader in circumstances which required a more
crusading, ideological role of him. Neither I nor anyone else was
smart enough to spot this at the time and gradually old values, old
patterns of behaviour were reasserted and rewarded. There can be
no effective transformation of an organization without heroes; the
ultimate paradox is that the comic mean can only be brought about
by the most melodramatic of leaders.

Finally, there remains the issue of emotions. The highly
charismatic leader may be such a powerful advocate that all are
swept up behind him or her, with little thought for their own
positions, but such circumstances are not the rule. Social actors are
psychologically attached to their current relationships, however
bizarre and unrewarding these may appear to outsiders. Disturbance is rarely embraced unless some advantage is discernible in it.
Tony and Eric were as outspoken as the rest about the
ineffectiveness of the executive team *before* the restructuring; after,
they were full of praise for the old order and the certainties it
provided them. They were not alone in this; other members of the
executive, exposed as they were to long and arduous sessions in
which they sought to articulate and clarify new ways of proceeding,
occasionally sought solace in how 'things used to be'. Emotion is
often experienced as overwhelming, as flooding out logical thought
in such circumstances. It was not unusual to find the group anxious
to cut off potentially threatening exploration: 'This kind of talk will
do us no good at all. We have to settle for what we have.' Refusing
to acknowledge that emotion is involved, encouraging routine

discussion, diverting attention to elaborate plans and schedules serves little or no purpose; the emotions do not disappear, although their psychological manifestations may be reduced.

I have written elsewhere[12] about emotions, but it is important to restate my position here. An emotion is a basic judgement about our selves, about where we stand in relation to our selves and those of others, about the realization or failure to realize our values and ideals. Paul's anger depicted in the first pages of this book is a judgement that he has been offended by George; George's shame is the judgement that he, as Finance Director, has performed badly. It is the invocation of a particular response, a script, which is taken to be appropriate to the circumstance. Sadness, guilt, anger, pride or whatever are all matters of judgement about situation, self and others.

The figures that George presents do not bring about emotional reactions; both George's and Paul's emotions are judgements about the import of them. The figures – or any other structure – are never in and of themselves sufficient for emotion. Emotions always, everywhere and inevitably involve personal evaluations of specific incidents. A change in definition and evaluation may entail a change in emotion. Emotions are the consequence of inter-pretations, not simply reactions to 'facts', still less the result of eruptions of feelings from within. George's 'shame' and 'guilt' may well be accompanied by perceptible difference in heart-rate, in breathing and perspiration, but if persuaded 'pride' is a more appropriate judgement, 'shame' will dissolve, leaving only the feelings. The emotion is the judgement, not the physiological state.

At times of significant transition, when matters of authority and fraternity are to the fore, emotions are likely to be high. If, as appears to be the case, I locate myself in terms of authority and fraternity, I am likely to experience attention to such features of my relations with others as potentially threatening. Discussion is thus likely to become 'emotional' and 'heated'. The display of emotion should alert us to the fact that judgement is being questioned and that there is thus everything to be gained in persisting in the exploration. If, as I have argued, organizations are held together (and apart) by emotions, my attempt at separating and reconstitut-ing the elements must venture into areas which hitherto have been beyond the pale. If emotions are judgements, then to better understand the display of feeling, we must discern its basis. Emotion can be comprehended as well as apprehended; the force of expression of it may well signal the necessity for careful but determined attempts to bottom it. Strong emotions may well characterize scripts which are particularly resistant to elucidation and revision; a lack of persistence may well be regretted later. Paul, Tony and Eric resisted strongly any attempts to clarify the nature of their authority relations whilst ostensibly claiming that they wished to resolve the issue. My attempts were met by anger and aggression, by blame and contempt. I desisted because I did not wish to embarrass or further discomfort Paul. The cost became obvious later. Feelings will be aroused in all such events; they should always be addressed, never avoided.

What this book celebrates beyond all else is dialogue. What I am looking for in the ideal executive is a social arrangement that builds and facilitates the expression of and reconciliation of disparate ideas. What I am seeking to promote through the process of change is also dialogue: about present arrangements, about beliefs, values, ideas *and* emotions. Nothing is beyond dialogue:

> Dialogue is the only way, not only in the vital questions of political order, but in all expressions of our being. Only by virtue of faith, however, does dialogue have power and meaning: by faith that I am only become truly myself when other men also become themselves.[13]

That this is no easy route, no shirking of responsibility, no soft option, I hope I have demonstrated in these pages.

> Anyone can run to excesses.
> It is easy to shoot past the mark.
> It is hard to stand firm in the middle.[14]

It is harder still when, to find the middle, one must first sound the extremities.

Epilogue

I cannot, of course, close on a note of regret, still less one of guilt. The essence of this book has been the emphasis upon acceptance, upon reconciliation of the ideal with the possible, upon finding the disappointing and the imperfect understandable. Paul and George must 'push on', so must I. It is disturbing and frustrating not to have done better, not to have got more than half a loaf, but all of us, at times, must avoid excessive expectation. I have not realized my dream of creating a world in which disparate and conflicting views are identified, explored and reconciled, but I have gone a considerable way towards that and, in doing so, have clarified my ideas and identified my goal: to enable more of us to assume a comic mean, an acceptance of diversity.

The world which I wish to see has a place for Paul and George, Alec and Hugh; it revels in all shades of opinion, most forms of behaviour and holds to no constant beyond that of civility: an identification of disparateness, an empathic appreciation of other positions, but a desire to transcend partisanship. I take such a stance to be essential to the successful prosecution of the executive process.

One final word. Over the past couple of years, Paul, George and the others have largely succeeded in reducing costs, identifying an appropriate strategy and moving towards its implementation; on the technical, functional side of the business, they have become even more proficient than they were before. As I have sought to indicate, however, technical proficiency is a necessary but not sufficient condition for company success. Something else is needed: an understanding of and skill in the executive process.

Notes

Prologue

1 A mixed bag, this lot. *Top Decisions*, a snappy title undercut by its
subtitle, *Strategic Decision Making in Organizations*, is written by a
clutch of people – Hickson, Butler, Cray, Mallory and Wilson –
and it shows. To quote the blurb: 'The book presents an
unparalleled breadth of information about the process of making
major decisions.' It is not a book of brilliant insights (nor does it
purport to be) and it is not a good read, but persevere and you too
can become an expert.

   Decision Making at the Top: The Shaping of Strategic Direction
covers similar ground but with a more impressionistic approach
(although based upon interviews). It is much less thorough and is
consequently easier to digest. Gordon Donaldson and Jay W.
Lorsch are experienced academic communicators, and although
apparently thrown by the notion that senior managers become
emotionally attached to ideas, nonetheless recover to present some
interesting views of belief systems and diversification. The diversification index they produce is silly but then so are most quantitative
indices; sensible managers should eschew algebraic formulations,
students have no choice but to embrace them enthusiastically if
they are to pass their examinations.

   The Executive Mind, edited by Suresh Srivastva and subtitled *New
Insights on Managerial Thought and Action*, results from a symposium
held at Case Western Reserve University in the early eighties. Like
many such compilations, it is very much a curate's egg; indeed,
some contributors are downright rank, but there is enough fresh
yolk about to make a nutritious meal for someone on a diet. Weick,
as always, is good value, as are Torbert, Friedlander, Argyris and
Srivastva himself.

Chapter 2

1   A word or two about models before I proceed to the substance of
    mine. Basically a model is a representation of the various aspects of a
    relatively complex and potentially confusing event or situation. A
    model is necessarily a simplification and, because of this, may not
    include all of the variables potentially relevant to the circumstance or
    event it purports to represent. It should, however, if it is a good
    model, include all of those variables which the model builder
    considers important because its value lies in its ability to abstract
    from reality in such a way that understanding, and predictions or
    outcomes, are possible. Models are analogies which each of us uses –
    wittingly or unwittingly – to clarify our thinking and guide our action.
    The primary use of a model – particularly that outlined in the
    following pages – is to describe and understand people, rela-
    tionships, events and situations; my model is, therefore, at once
    descriptive and explanatory. Later, when I come to talk of effecting
    change, the model used will be predictive and prescriptive, but these
    delights must wait.
        The problem with models is the very range and diversity of them;
    social science has produced a multitude of descriptions and
    explanations which appear to have very little connection between
    them. Traditional approaches are so diverse that most appear to
    address but a small and relatively insignificant part of the 'reality'
    with which we are confronted, while those with a seemingly wider
    scope appear to be mutually exclusive: one is either an interactionist
    or a functionalist, an adherent of exchange theory or a Marxist.
        Part of this diversity and confusion is explained by the relative
    youth and immaturity of social science as a subject. Part of the rivalry
    may be simple bloody mindedness – in a new and rapidly developing
    field, everyone wishes to make a name and the most effective way of
    doing that is to be perverse, or at least different. Part, however, is the
    product of particular and peculiar emphases. It is possible to
    distinguish at least four levels of analysis in the study of behaviour in
    organizations. The first is concerned exclusively with 'psychological'
    or 'intrapersonal' processes: what happens in an organization is
    depicted as the result of the way an individual construes and
    organizes his or her experiences of that world. Very popular in
    business biographies (more so in ghosted autobiographies), the
    'I-got-to-the-top-to-prove-to-my-father-I-could-do-it',   or
    whatever, is a clearly identifiable approach. A second kind of

description and explanation looks beyond the individual to the dynamics of 'interpersonal' and 'intrasituational' processes. This approach clearly acknowledges the importance of other people and of circumstances in our action and is very popular with academics. If one assumes, as is so often assumed at this level of explanation, that people are interchangeable, then one can construct all kinds of descriptions and explanations. Behaviour can be seen as a result of group forces – teams can and have been constructed on the basis of the need for particular types of mutuality and/or skill – and under experimental and laboratory conditions, behaviour can be manipulated and predicted. A third type of explanation recognizes that extrasituational factors may be of consequence in interactions; no one comes naked to the conference table, we are each located on a point within a structure of power and status and these attributes affect definitions, relations and actions. Finally, a fourth kind of explanation begins much further out, a long way from the individual, with an analysis of broad concepts covering society in general and attempts to show how, for example, ideologies lead to different ways of construing events and, consequently, to different patterns of behaviour.

It is, of course, nonsense to claim that each and every model can be assigned to one or other of these types of analysis; there is overlap in many of the approaches, but the distinction is useful in that it helps to see the peculiar emphasis of particular approaches. The first approach – the intrapersonal – is essentially reductionist; it attempts to describe and explain events in terms of non-social factors. The last, behaviour as a consequence of ideological beliefs, appears to have little or no place for the individual; actions are the products of values and even historical inevitabilities. For example, it could be argued that there is a widespread belief that people (by and large) get their just deserts: that reward and punishment, positive and negative sanctions, are not distributed by chance. It might be noted, to be sure, that this belief is strongest amongst those currently enjoying positive sanctions, but is present even amongst the less favoured. Thus the explanation would hold that it is acceptable to large sections of a particular society to ignore or perhaps even scorn the disadvantaged, since they clearly deserve their fate. The individuals doing the ignoring or the scorning are not at fault in any way, are not responsible for their actions, their behaviour is no more than a reflection of the dominant ideology. At its extreme, of course, such an explanation robs the social actor of any individuality at all; from within such a model, what each of us does is the product of forces beyond our control.

Put directly, there has been and continues to be a division between those who see behaviour as essentially the product of relatively independent individual processes and those who see it as a product of social and collective forces. The view adopted throughout this book is that some way of articulating these two perspectives needs to be found; it is clear to me, as it is to a great number of others, that social and collective forces can only occur through the actions of individuals; action is coordinated, it does not simply happen spontaneously. It is equally clear that individual definitions (what is going on here, what is to be my part in it) and actions are affected by social structure and ideology which generate and guide individual activities. A socialist society has different consequences for the individual than a capitalist one; a Protestant ethic constrasts sharply with a Hindu one and has profoundly different implications for the individual. The former stresses salvation through individual effort, the latter through the notion of *dharma* emphasizes obligation and duty and discourages social mobility. But our behaviour is not *determined* by such macro considerations. Many people have escaped from the press of their societies.

Behaviour is best seen as the product of individual and social factors, just as area is the product of length and breadth. This is easy to say and simple to write, but extraordinarily difficult to articulate. I make no claims that the perspective advocated over the next few pages achieves this articulation. At best it can be described as eclectic which we are told 'in ancient use [is] an epithet of a class of philosophers who selected such doctrines as pleased them in every school'. My approach may be said to be eclectic; broad, not exclusive and borrowing ideas from various sources. My model embraces descriptions and analyses from all four of the types adduced above and, like the proverbial thieving magpie, I take bright, shiny ideas from a number of psychological, social psychological and sociological traditions.

Much of this material arises directly from Wilhelm Doise's *Levels of Exploration in Social Psychology*. The arguments concerning the primacy of individuals or society can be found in virtually any introductory text and are tiresome. A fine resolution of them is to be found in Giddens (1984), but you have to be really interested to plough through that kind of material: scholarly, precise, articulate and immensely detailed.

2 This list is by no means exhaustive; it simply indicates those whom I know to have influenced my ideas. There are likely to be others whose views are now so sedimented with my own that I can no longer

distinguish their contribution. There are some, Randall Collins for example, whose contributions are so specific that they are picked up in the text and acknowledged explicitly in the notes. By far the most important influence upon my thoughts, however, have been novelists, playwrights and literary critics, many of whom go unsung in these pages and are no doubt grateful for that.

3 Just as I said. Randall Collins, *Three Sociological Traditions*, a fine book focusing upon the development of three schools of sociological thought: 'conflict tradition', 'ritual solidarity tradition' and the 'microinteractionist tradition', to which I claim some allegiance. Much of what I have to say about pragmatism derives from this source, although I did take the trouble to read Peirce himself, in *Philosophical Writings of Peirce* edited by J. Bucher, and of him in Schneider's *A History of American Philosophy*. Lewis and Smith's *American Sociology and Pragmatism* is also of value.

4 William James slips in here as a founding father of pragmatism. His main point was not that ideas are to be taken as copies of external objects but rather that truth is a form of action. If ideas work, that is good enough. Collins (1985) notes that he was 'rather a lightweight philosopher' and, presumably, easily supplanted by the 'real intellectual leader' of pragmatism, Charles Sanders Peirce who, incidentally and probably wisely, never published a book or held academic office. He was my kind of chap, coining all kinds of lovely phrases: agapasticism, idioscopy, fallibilism, synechism, illation and, delightfully, 'the Chorising, Cyclory, Periproxy, and Apexing of Space'. He was a joker but a good one and, as I will argue later, there is always a place for a good fool.

5 Another of Charles Sanders Peirce's thoughts and one increasingly confirmed by latter-day psychologists and philosophers. A splendid volume written in this vein, *The Passions* by Robert C. Solomon, strongly influenced *Power and Performance in Organizations* and underpins the present book.

6 Quote from Randall Collins (1985).

7 The literature on the interactionist tradition has taken off in recent years. The best general introductory texts to read are Lauer and Handel, *Social Psychology: The Theory and Application of Symbolic Interactionism*; Heiss, *The Social Psychology of Interaction*; Hewitt, *Self and Society: A Symbolic Interactionist Social Psychology*; together with Berger's *Invitation to Sociology*. Collins's essay is good value in *Three Sociological Traditions*, and Blumer's *Symbolic Interactionism* is simply indispensable.

8 One of the great mysteries of publishing is how good books, seminal

texts, go out of print. *Men Who Manage* by Dalton is not available nor, more to the point, is McCall and Simmons's *Identities and Interactions*. Beg, borrow or steal it – the most you will get is a suspended sentence and it's a reasonable price to pay for an important text.

9   Mead was another genius who failed to get his ideas down on paper; his students put them together under the title *Mind, Self and Society*. The result is a somewhat jumbled presentation of thoughts, difficult to read and, occasionally, difficult to comprehend, but a volume which had and continues to have an impact upon scholars from a range of disciplines.

10   The same book as before – keep chasing it.

11   Much of this material, of course, has previously appeared in *Power and Performance in Organizations* which, in turn, draws heavily upon Bedrich Baumann's impressive text, *Imaginative Participation: The Career of an Organizing Concept in a Multidisciplinary Context*.

12   The late Erving Goffman, an extraordinary scholar and effective writer who, although grossly overrated (his major work, *Presentation of Self*, purports to erect a dramaturgical framework but he shows next to no awareness of such a frame), is nonetheless a major figure. *Frame Analysis* is another of his books that, although somewhat heavy going, is valuable.

13   Goffman, *Presentation of Self*.

14   The notion of altercasting comes from Weinstein and Deutschberger's article, 'Tasks, Bargains and Identities in Social Interaction'. The quote is from Peter Hall's paper, 'A Symbolic Interactionist Analysis of Politics'.

15   McCall and Simmons again.

16   The thing about 'working agreements' is their essential temporary character; they exist only to be changed. In fact, as I will shortly argue, temporary agreements are the exception rather than the rule; many, perhaps most, of our interactions follow patterns which appear to have obtained for generations. Negotiation and bargaining are more honoured in the breach than the observance.

17   Underlying all of this, of course, is the notion of exchange. Interaction may be seen as a function of what each person gets out of a relationship. All behaviour is subject to the same bottom line: profit. You may well boggle at the thought that there is a price for everything and every one of us has a price, just as you may remain unconvinced by a theory, behaviourist in essence, which places such a high reliance on *rational* behaviour. Watch this space; the criticism is reserved for a later chapter. What is pertinent is the mention of

'negotiating order' which surfaces in this chapter. It is an important idea which, for reasons of the flow of argument, I do not do justice to in the text itself. The key book and one which must be read is *Negotiations* by Anselm Strauss (1978). He holds that all social orders are in some respects negotiated orders and uses three concepts to outline his ideas: negotiation, negotiation context and structural context. The first refers to the strategies used by participants (something of the flavour is contained in the chapter to which these notes refer); the second concerns the relevant features of the setting which affect the course of the interaction (dimensions of power and status which are dealt with later); and the third concept deals with the larger circumstances (state, law, social class or whatever) within which the negotiation takes place. Strauss emphasizes that contexts affect negotiations and that negotiations affect contexts. Structural features condition the way people act *and* the way people act eventually and perhaps indirectly influences structures.

What I pick up in this section is the tentative and temporal aspects of interaction:

> the shared agreements, the binding contracts which constitute the grounds for an expectable, non-surprising, taken-for-granted, even ruled orderliness are not binding and shared for all time. Contracts, understandings, agreements, rules – all have appended to them a temporal clause.

A good review of negotiated order theory and research is that provided by Day and Day (1977), 'A Review of the Current State of Negotiated Order Theory'.

18 Collins again: 'Peirce, 20 years or more before Freud, was conceiving of mental processes as operating unconsciously as long as the habits of connection are firmly established and nothing happens to disturb the smooth flow of inference. On the other hand, we become highly conscious of something when we become emotionally aroused about it; in fact the emotion is simply the particular type of disturbance we were experiencing in the flow of inference.' I agree with the first part, not the second; most interaction is emotional, what disturbs it is a threat to authority and fraternity which produces another emotion. For further discussion, see later pages.

19 The idea of scripts comes specifically from the work of Roger Schank, *Scripts, Plans, Goals and Understanding*, co-authored with Robert Abelson. Further discussion of it occurs in *Organization Analysis and Development*, which I edited, and in *The Thinking*

Organization edited by Sims, Gioia and associates, notably the essay by Gioia, 'Symbols, Scripts and Sensemaking: Creating Meaning in Organizational Experience'. Karl Weick makes use of it also in his paper in a recent text edited by Jay Lorsch, *Handbook of Organizational Behavior*.

20 This keeps getting quoted, probably because it is so succinct. I do not know its origin and I don't particularly care: nothing else from Lippman is ever quoted so, whatever the source, it is probably not worth reading.

21 The following extract from Nobbs's *The Death of Reginald Perrin* is probably worth a mention in this context:

Joan ushered Mr Campbell-Lewiston in. He was wearing a lightweight grey suit and was carrying a fawn German raincoat. When he smiled Reggie noticed that his teeth were yellow.

'How are things going in Germany?' said Reggie.

'It's tough,' said Mr Campbell-Lewiston. 'Jerry's very conservative. He doesn't go in for convenience foods as much as we do.'

'Good for him.'

'Yes, I suppose so, but I mean it makes our job more difficult.'

'More of a challenge,' said Reggie.

Joan entered with a pot of coffee on a tray. There were three biscuits each – a bourbon, a rich tea and a custard cream.

'There are some isolated regional breakthroughs,' said Mr Campbell-Lewiston. 'Some of the mousses are holding their own in the Rhenish Palatinate, and the flans are cleaning up in Schleswig-Holstein.'

'Oh good, that's very comforting to know,' said Reggie. 'And what about the Bakewell tart mix, is it going like hot cakes?'

'Not too well, I'm afraid.'

Reggie poured out two cups of coffee and handed one to his visitor. Mr Campbell-Lewiston took four lumps of sugar.

'And how about the tinned treacle pudding – is that proving sticky?'

'Oh very good. Treacle tart sticky. You're a bit of a wag,' said Mr Campbell-Lewiston, and he laughed yellowly.

Suddenly the penny dropped.

'Good God,' said Reggie, 'Campbell-Lewiston. I thought the name was familiar. Campbell-Lewiston, E.L. Ruttingstagg. The small bore rifle team.'

'Of course. Goofy Per . . . R.I. Perrin.'

They shook hands.

'You're doing pretty well for yourself,' said Reggie.

'You too,' said E.L. Campbell-Lewiston.

'You were a nauseous little squirt in those days,' said Reggie.
E.L. Campbell-Lewiston drew in his breath sharply.

'Thank heavens for small bores, for small bores grow bigger every day,' said Reggie.

'What?'

'I really must congratulate you on the work you're doing in Germany,' said Reggie. 'Do you remember the time you bit me in the changing room?'

'I don't remember that.'

'I think you've done amazingly well with those flans in Schleswig-Holstein,' said Reggie. 'And now what I'd like you to do is pave the way for our new range of exotic ices. There are three flavours – mango delight, cumquat surprise and strawberry and lychee ripple.'

'I can't believe it. I've never bitten anyone.'
Reggie stood up and spoke dynamically.

'Aren't you listening?' he said, 'I'm talking about our new range of ice creams.'

'Oh, yes. Sorry,' said E.L. Campbell-Lewiston.

'I'd like you to try it out in a typical German town,' said Reggie.
'Are there any typical German towns?'

'All German towns are typical,' said E.L. Campbell-Lewiston.
Reggie sipped his coffee thoughtfully, and said nothing. E.L. Campbell-Lewiston waited uneasily.

'Is there any particular way you want me to handle the new ice creams?' he asked at length.

'Wanking much these days, are you?' asked Reggie.

'I beg your pardon?'

'We used to call you the phantom wanker. No wonder you could never hit the bloody target.'
E.L. Campbell-Lewiston stood up. His face was flushed.

'I didn't come here to be insulted like that,' he said.

'Sorry,' said Reggie. 'I'll insult you like this, then. You don't clean your teeth properly, you slovenly sod.'

'Just who do you think you are?' said E.L. Campbell-Lewiston.

'I think I'm the man in charge of the new exotic ices project,' said Reggie. 'I'm the man who's expecting you to take Germany by storm, and I have every confidence you will. I was tremendously impressed by your article on the strengths and limitations of market research in the *International Deep Freeze News*.'

'Oh thank you.'

They stood up and Reggie handed Mr Campbell-Lewiston his raincoat.

'Yes, I found your analysis of the chance element inherent in any random sample very persuasive.'

'I hoped it was all right.'

At the door E.L. Campbell-Lewiston turned and offered Reggie his hand.

'Er ... all this ... I mean, is it some kind of new middle management technique?' he asked.

'That's right,' said Reggie. 'It's the new thing. Try it out on the Germans.'

22 James G. March and Herbert A. Simon, *Organizations*, in 1958. A golden oldie, full of wit, wisdom and insight.

23 By me, no less, in a related text published by Wiley, *Interactions and Interventions in Organizations*.

24 Generations of writers and consultants have made managers, even senior managers, nervous about taking decisions. They 'know' that they must not act without reflection, they 'know' that they need as much information as possible before deciding on a course of action, leave alone implementing it; thus rational models of choice and decision robs them of decisiveness. Current scripts at executive level may actually institutionalize search analysis and reflection at the expense of action; executives reflect unreflectively about the processes they sustain.

25 A number of the points I make in this chapter are informed by the ideas of William H. Starbuck (sounds like the hero of a space epic) and in particular 'Organizations as Action Generators', in which he flirts with but never actually embraces the dramaturgical perspective.

26 In such circumstances, it appears that no one wishes to go beyond the facile. Derek is happy to have an agreement, however tacky, and the others are not sufficiently concerned to deny him his activity. At one level, therefore, all is agreed, at another, nothing really is and all is still in the air. It could be that a great number of social scripts have this quality, a perceived level of importance such that few question them or invest energy in them. On the other hand, should Derek's plans involve a perceived threat to authority or fraternity, should he for example advocate worker directors, a seat on the executive for the catering assistant, then others will engage with him.

27 *Waiting for Godot* by Samuel Beckett.

28 The broad background for this section on improvisation is to be found in 'Cognitive Processes in Improvisation' by Jeff Pressing,

whose main interest lies in music. Alistair Preston (1987), also with an interest in music (jazz), provides an insightful comment upon improvising order in organizations.

29 In *Organizations as Theatre: A Social Psychology of Dramatic Appearances*, with Michael Overington. See also *Power and Performance in Organizations* (1986).

30 Theodore D. Kemper (1978) has a useful review of related ideas pointing out that his model (similar to my own) is not a novelty. He cites Freedman, Leary, Ossorio and Coffrey (1951), Leary (1957), Brown (1965), Bales (1970) and a number of others of lesser importance.

31 The quotation is from Herbert Simons's 'The Carrot and Stick as Handmaidens of Persuasion in Conflict Situations'.

32 This rash statement is a direct consequence of reading and rereading Richard Sennett, in particular his essay *Authority* (1980). It appears that he may now have abandoned academia for different groves; his novels, particularly *Palais Royal*, are also well worth reading. Much of what I have to say in these pages about authority, fraternity and bonding derives directly from Sennett.

33 Bakunin, quoted in Sennett (1980).

34 Sennett (1980).

35 Sennett (1980) has fraternity as a main characteristic of human interaction but devotes little time to it. Unfortunately, a promised essay on it has yet to materialize.

36 Sennett again, I'm afraid. Not, however, a direct crib, just a coincidence of ideas. I read Collins (1981) and Kemper (1978) before I came across Sennett who is, as it turns out, not very forthcoming on emotions but has a felicitous interpretation of 'bonding', which I am more than happy to appropriate.

37 Randall Collins (1981) makes out a strong case for emotional bonding in his seminal paper, 'On the Microfoundations of Macrosociology', hardly a catchy title but worth a read, particularly for the stress he places upon 'emotional energies' which he sees as the most crucial 'mechanism' (oh dear) in all social processes.

38 Collins (1981).

39 See also *Organizations as Theatre* (1987).

40 Collins again, this time *Three Sociological Traditions* (1985).

Chapter 3

1 The categorization has been influenced by my observations, my discussions with colleagues and by my reading. Sennett (1980) remains

the strongest influence but, at several removes, the ideas of the Tavistock School, notably those of A.K. Rice, are present in these pages. See in particular, *Exploring Individual and Organizational Boundaries*, edited by W. Gordon Lawrence (1979). Although of a somewhat different orientation, the ideas of Dorothy Stock Whitaker and Morton A. Lieberman (1964), particularly the notion of 'focal conflict', have impressed themselves upon me. Kenwyn K. Smith and D.M. Berg (1987), in 'full collaboration', have produced a very interesting text, *Paradoxes of Group Life*, which has also been of considerable influence upon this categorization. It contains a number of notions and, although not explicitly stated, clearly reflects a 'comic' or balanced approach to life in organizations. For an explanation of this sentence, you will need to continue reading
. . .

2 This extract appears in *Organizations as Theatre* (1987).
3 This turns out to be one of the paradoxes that Smith and Berg (1987) also pick up. The supreme difficulty for an executive group is that it must expose differences, enhance rather than inhibit conflict, *before* it can attempt to reconcile different positions, *but*, in promoting differences, it fears that it will cease to be a group. Nonetheless, its very success depends upon walking the wire above the cage of lions it is simultaneously poking!
4 This represents a difference in tone from other scenes involving the group. How it was achieved will be discussed later.
5 Trust is one of those words used as a weapon in some areas of human interaction, as a talisman in others. 'You do not trust me' can be said in a hurt tone, challenging you to declare it to be true. More often than not it provokes the response 'Of course I do' which, theoretically, opens the way for further exploration of the relationship. Theoretically, because often 'Of course I do' is secretly qualified by 'but I will watch you like a hawk'. I am using it here as the quality of 'having faith or confidence' in one's colleagues, faith and confidence that they will not take advantage of any vulnerability I may reveal in owning a particular attribute or drawing attention to an aspect of our interaction.
6 See, in particular comments in Whitaker and Lieberman (1964).
7 Smith and Berg (1987) have an extended discussion of various 'paradoxes'.
8 Smith and Berg (1987) again, but the ideas of leadership and followership, authority and authorizing, have a longer pedigree; see, in particular, my *Power and Performance in Organizations* (1986). This section is also indebted to Sennett (1980).

9   Taken from field notes and recordings made by the author.
10 Sennett (1980).
11 Parts of this material appear in Clegg, Kemp and Legge (1985). Like all other extracts, it is the product of recording and/or field notes edited for inclusion in this text.
12 It is, of course, a moot point as to whether there is any need for a *team* approach. Tony could argue (and did) that his role as sanctioned by the Independent Broadcasting Authority made him and him alone answerable for the quality of programmes. He may well have seen Neville's desire to inculcate team spirit as a direct attack upon his role and authority.

Chapter 4

1   Lifted from Alonzo McDonald, 'Conflict at the Summit: A Deadly Game', *Harvard Business Review* (1972).
2   I could fill a book with such comments; a glance at the business pages will amply confirm the point, as will the reading of business biographies.
3   Taken from field notes made at the time.
4   This section of the book is clearly and heavily influenced by my interest in drama and theatre-going. In particular, I draw heavily upon Dawson (1970), Brooks (1984), Hornby (1977), Smith (1973) and Heilman (1978). The last has many a felicitous turn of phrase which has brought delight to me and influenced my own style in these pages. The idea of the comic mean derives directly from him although, of course, its application in a non-theatrical context is my own.
    The idea also surfaces in Joseph Brodsky's (1986) collection of essays, *Less than One*, itself commented upon in *The Spectator* (26 September 1987):

> He [Brodsky] comes near, for example, to defining one of the signs that marks a poet – creatures he would clearly put near the centre of any concept of 'civilisation'. He is talking of his relief that he went to prison rather than into the army: 'My hatred's centre of gravity, in other words, wasn't dispersed into some foreign capitalist nowhere; it wasn't even hatred. The damned trait of understanding, and then forgiving everybody, which started when I was in school, fully blossomed in prison. I don't think I even hated my KGB interrogators; I tended to

absolve even them (good-for-nothing has a family to feed, etc.).' This is more than sympathy, it is closer to Coleridge's 'empathy', to 'negative capability', to Keats's capacity to enter into the sparrow pecking among the gravel. It is, or it should be, at the heart of 'civilization', yet it is the despair and bewilderment of those who maintain and control the means of civilized life, policemen and politicians. This is a world of one-sided arguments, confrontations, the making and impos-ing of distinctions. The two ways of looking at the world do not understand each other at all (although they are mutually dependent) which is why in totalitarian regimes the poets have to go.

5 George Bernard Shaw, *The Doctor's Dilemma*.
6 Effective executive *teams*, of course, are ones in which no one member dominates. As I have attempted to show, dominance will eventually produce rebellion.
7 The melodramatic stance on the other hand, of course, claims just this – that I can take on the task and win. It is much more splendid than the kind of wishy-washy compromise that I am suggesting. We live in uncompromising times where the benefits of individualism are extolled daily. I remain unconvinced.
8 Appearances, however, are deceptive. These are scripts, they are powerful influences, but they do not *determine* our behaviour. I shape and am shaped by my behaviour and that of others.
9 Quote from Peter Berger, *Invitation to Sociology: A Humanistic Perspective*.
10 By page 113 he is really rubbing it in – he *appears* to be claiming that we *are* the parts we play.
11 George Herbert Mead (see chapter 2). See also *Mead* by John D. Baldwin (1986).
12 G.H. Mead, again, at least as interpreted by Charles Morris (1934).
13 and 14: see note 10. There appears no possibility of escape from the view as ourselves as puppets with the strings pulled by society.
15 Georg Simmel. For those interested in a master thinker, see Lawrence (1976).
16 The quote is taken from his essay, 'On the Theory of Theatrical Performance', reproduced in Burns and Burns (1973).
17 The notion of possession is picked up in *Organizations as Theatre*.
18 Simmel in Burns and Burns (1973).
19 A clear statement of the newer, more creative perspective on sociology from Cuzzort and King (1976).

20 This time Berger and Luckmann (1967), *The Social Construction of Reality*.

21 See also *Interactions and Interventions in Organizations* (1978). The term 'metatheatrical' is lifted from Abel (1963), although here used in a different manner.

22 Just as linguistic as metalanguage.

23 Consultants make a very good living from such ways. The best academic approach to the effecting of change (and in this context, I do not take academic to be pejorative) is that elaborated by Argyris in a series of books. I am particularly impressed by *Strategy, Change and Defensive Routines* (1985).

24 Anton C. Zijderveld (1982).

25 Zijderveld (1982).

26 Power in this context is taken to equate with naked force.

27 Just as change agents occasionally imbue us with a feeling that this time we will really make it, really bring it off.

28 The quote – lovely, isn't it? – comes from *Piers Plowman*, written by William Langland in the fourteenth century.

Chapter 5

1 I dealt with interpretation at some length in *Organizations as Theatre* (1987).

2 Much of what I have to say in this section derives from Hornby (1977).

3 This point echoes one made in the prologue in which I argued that all attempts to reproduce interaction imply some level of creativity; that favoured by those interested in linguistic analysis may be slight (the choice of passage, the elimination of physical gestures, context, etc.) but it is, nevertheless, editorial in that it is a selection of material. My own approach is much more selective, much more shaped.

4 Hornby (1977).

5 These criteria derive directly from Stein Haugom Olsen (1978), whose work underpins much of the rest of this discussion. The text in which these criteria appear is *The Structure of Literary Understanding* (which is marginally more readable than most sociology texts, but it's a close call).

6 Were I to provide further examples, they would of necessity focus upon authority and fraternity, since my selection would be guided by my perception; each of us has our filters, mine are, in this case,

explicit; others may perceive other features in the passages I have reproduced. Feel free.

Chapter 6

1 For reviews of the impact of interventions in groups, see in particular Friedlander and Brown (1974); and Woodman and Sherwood (1980). Goodman and associates (1986) provide a relatively stimulating discussion of the design of effective work teams and their extensive bibliography could save you a great deal of time and effort.

2 The issue of leadership has spawned a vast literature. The most recent work is that of Schein (1985), Bennis and Nanus (1985), and Tichy and Devanna (1986). What they have to say is broadly in line with the kind of position I adopt in this book, although the terminology and emphases may be different. Burns (1978) provides the most thorough survey around and, acknowledged or otherwise, is the source of much written in the eighties. Hunt et al. (1984) provide 'new perspectives' – a book of conference papers, most of which are hardly worth the print costs and some definitely not.

3 For further comments on the decline of the role of the fool brought about by his institutionalization, see Anton Zijderveld (1982).

4 Zijderveld (1982).

5 This was a development I had not anticipated but found myself enjoying. As Alec, Hugh, Derek, George and the rest talked to me, I convinced myself (with great ease) that it would be to the advantage of all if I were to carry the messages. As Hamlet's uncle, Claudius, had it, there is a divinity that doth hedge about a king (or words to that effect) and there certainly is a pleasurable *frisson* to be had from being a confidant of the most powerful man or woman in an organization. I ought to have known better and behaved differently, but I didn't.

6 Zijderveld (1982).

7 The quotation (as if you needed to be reminded) is from a speech of Viola's in *Twelfth Night*, Act III, Scene I. It does, of course, make nonsense of the role of the fool who needs to go beyond the bounds of the acceptable. He needs, therefore, to check at feathers, but occasionally (and the judgement is all) continue.

8 The quote is from Erving Goffman (1983), who in all circumstances is worth reading. He is much less boring than the average sociologist, with a wide range of sources and a happy turn of phrase. He is much quoted by everyone but, unfortunately, had little influence on

mainstream social thought and almost none on what passes for thinking about organization and management.

9   I have been involved in all three kinds of response. The most frequent is to ignore the feedback, to promise to read it and 'get back to you' – nothing happens and, despite calls to discover what is happening, nothing does. The snipping out of 'sensitive sections' of the report has also been suggested to me, with one chief executive even going so far as to strike out all negative references to himself whilst highlighting the few positive comments in a day-glow pen. I have also experienced the kind of CEO who 'guesses' who said what, writes names and initials alongside comments and seeks, none too subtly, to have his views confirmed. One, subsequently removed from his position, declared to the respondents that he 'knew who said what' and would be 'speaking to them individually' about their 'misunderstandings'; this caused a degree of panic, rapidly dissolved on checking with me.

10 See previous comments upon the literature of leadership. This passage owes a great deal to the views of Peter Seiderberg (1984), a specialist in political theory.

11 Burns (1978).

12 See *Power and Performance in Organizations*.

13 Karl Jaspers, cited in Srivastva and associates, *Executive Power*. Anything by Suresh Srivastva is worth reading, and his concluding chapter in this book (with Frank J. Barrett) is up to his usually high standard. *The Executive Mind* (1983) is of a similar quality.

14 *Canto XIII* by Ezra Pound (1967). A Confucian perspective often to be found in Pound who in other respects is a man of extremes. For Confucian perspectives which accord with much of what I have outlined here, see Li Fu Chen (1986).

References

Abel, L. (1963). *Metatheatre*. New York: Basic Books.

Argyris, C. (1985). *Strategy, Change and Defensive Routines*. Marshfield: Pitman.

Baldwin, J.D. (1986). *George Herbert Mead: A Unifying Theory for Sociology*. Newbury Park: Sage.

Bales, R.F. (1970). *Interaction Process Analysis*. Cambridge, Mass.: Addison-Wesley.

Baumann, B. (1975). *Imaginative Participation: The Career of an Organizing Concept in a Multidisciplinary Context*. The Hague: Martinus Nijhoff.

Beckett, S. (1987). *Waiting for Godot*. Basingstoke: Macmillan.

Bennis, W. and Nanus, B. (1985). *Leaders: The Strategies for Taking Charge*. New York: Harper and Row.

Berger, P. (1963). *Invitation to Sociology: A Humanistic Perspective*. Harmondsworth: Penguin.

Berger, P. and Luckmann, T. (1967). *The Social Construction of Reality*. New York: Doubleday Anchor.

Blumer, H. (1969). *Symbolic Interactionism: Perspective and Method*. Englewood Cliffs, NJ: Prentice-Hall.

Brodsky, J. (1986). *Less Than One*. New York: Viking.

Brooks, P. (1984). *The Melodramatic Imagination*. New York: Columbia University Press.

Brown, R. (1965). *Social Psychology*. New York: Free Press.

Bucher, J. (ed.) (1940). *Philosophical Writings of Peirce*. New York: Dover.

Burns, E. and Burns, T. (1973). *Sociology of Literature and Drama*. Harmondsworth: Penguin.

Burns, J. McG. (1978). *Leadership*. New York: Harper and Row.

Clegg, C., Kemp, N. and Legge, K. (1985). *Case Studies in Organizational Behaviour*. London: Harper and Row.

Collins, R. (1981). 'On the Microfoundations of Macrosociology', *American Journal of Sociology* 86, 984–1014.

Collins, R. (ed.) (1985). *Three Sociological Traditions: Selected Readings.* New York: Oxford University Press.

Cuzzort, R.P. and King, E.W. (1976). *Humanity and Modern Social Thought.* Hinsdale, Illinois: The Dryden Press.

Dalton, M. (1959). *Men Who Manage.* New York: Wiley.

Dawson, S.W. (1970). *Drama and the Dramatic.* London: Methuen.

Day, R.A. and Day, J.V. (1977). 'A Review of the Current State of Negotiated Order Theory', *Sociological Quarterly* 18, 126–42.

Doise, W. (1986). *Levels of Exploration in Social Psychology.* Cambridge: Cambridge University Press.

Donaldson, G. and Lorsch, J.W. (1983). *Decision Making at the Top: The Shaping of Strategic Direction.* New York: Basic Books.

Freedman, M.B., Leary, T., Ossorio, A.G. and Coffrey, H.S. (1951). 'The Interpersonal Dimension of Personality', *Journal of Personality* 20, 143–161.

Friedlander, F. and Brown, L.D. (1974). 'Organization Development', in M.R. Rosenzweig and L.W. Porter (eds), *Annual Review of Psychology Volume 25*, Palo Alto: Annual Reviews.

Giddens, A. (1984). *The Constitution of Society.* Cambridge: Polity Press.

Goffman, E. (1959). *The Presentation of Self in Everyday Life.* New York: Doubleday Anchor.

Goffman, E. (1974). *Frame Analysis: An Essay on the Organization of Experience.* Harmondsworth: Penguin.

Goffman, E. (1983). 'The Interaction Order', *American Sociological Review* 48, 1–17.

Goodman P.S. and associates (1986). *Designing Effective Work Groups.* San Francisco: Jossey Bass.

Hall, P. (1972). 'A Symbolic Interactionist Analysis of Politics', *Sociological Inquiry* 42, 35–75.

Heilman, R.B. (1978). *The Ways of the World.* Seattle: University of Washington Press.

Heiss, J. (1981). *The Social Psychology of Interaction.* Englewood Cliffs, NJ: Prentice-Hall.

Hewitt, J.P. (1984). *Self and Society: A Symbolic Interactionist Social Psychology*, 3rd edn. Boston: Allyn and Bacon.

Hickson, D.J., Butler, R.J., Cray, D., Mallory, G.P. and Wilson, D.C. (1985). *Top Decisions: Strategic Decision Making in Organizations.* Oxford: Basil Blackwell.

Hornby, R. (1977). *Script into Performance.* Austin: University of Texas Press.

Hunt, J.G., Hosking, D.-M., Schriesheim, C.A. and Stewart, R. (1984). *Leaders and Managers: International Perspectives on Managerial Behaviour and Leadership.* Oxford: Pergamon Press.

Iacocca, L. (with Novak, W.) (1985). *Iacocca: An Autobiography*. London: Sidgwick and Jackson.

Kemper, T.D. (1978). *A Social Interactional Theory of Emotions*. New York: Wiley.

Langland, W. *Piers Plowman*, 1972 edn. Oxford: Oxford University Press.

Lauer, R.H. and Handel, W.H. (1977). *Social Psychology: The Theory and Application of Symbolic Interactionism*. Boston: Houghton Mifflin.

Lawrence, P.A. (1976). *Georg Simmel: Sociologist and European*. Sunbury-on-Thames: Nelson.

Lawrence, W.G. (ed.) (1979). *Exploring Individual and Organizational Boundaries: A Tavistock Open Systems Approach*. Chichester: Wiley.

Leary, T. (1957). *The Interpersonal Diagnosis of Personality*. New York: Ronald.

Lewis, J.D. and Smith, R.L. (1980). *American Sociology and Pragmatism*. Chicago: University of Chicago Press.

Li Fu Chen (1986). *The Confucian Way*. London: Kegan Paul.

McCall, G.J. and Simmons, J.L. (1978). *Identities and Interactions*. New York: Free Press.

McDonald, A. (1972). 'Conflict at the Summit: a Deadly Game', *Harvard Business Review*, March/April, 59–68.

Mangham, I.L. (1978). *Interactions and Interventions in Organizations*. Chichester: Wiley.

Mangham, I.L. (1986). *Power and Performance in Organizations: An Exploration of Executive Process*. Oxford: Basil Blackwell.

Mangham, I.L. (ed.) (1987). *Organization Analysis and Development: A Social Construction of Organizational Behaviour*. Chichester: Wiley.

Mangham, I.L. and Overington, M.A. (1987). *Organizations as Theatre: A Social Psychology of Dramatic Appearances*. Chichester: Wiley.

March, J.G. and Simon, H.A. (1958). *Organizations*. New York: Wiley.

Mead, G.H. (1934). *Mind, Self and Society*. Chicago: University of Chicago Press.

Morris, C.W. (1934). Introduction to G.H. Mead, *Mind, Self and Society*, Chicago: University of Chicago Press.

Nobbs, D. (1975). *The Death of Reginald Perrin*. London: Gollancz.

Olsen, S.H. (1978). *The Structure of Literary Understanding*. Cambridge: Cambridge University Press.

Pound, E. (1967). *Selected Cantos*. London: Faber and Faber.

Pressing, J. (1984). 'Cognitive Processes in Improvisation', in R. Crozier (ed.), *Cognitive Processes in the Perception of Art*, Amsterdam: North Holland.

Preston, A.M. (1987). 'Improvising Order', in I.L. Mangham (ed.), *Organization Analysis and Development*. Chichester: Wiley.

Schank, R. and Abelson, R. (1977). *Scripts, Plans, Goals and Understanding.* Hillsdale, NJ: Lawrence Erlbaum Associates.

Schein, E.H. (1985). *Organizational Culture and Leadership.* San Francisco: Jossey Bass.

Schneider, H.W. *A History of American Philosophy.* Livingston, NJ: Orient Book Distributors.

Seiderberg, P.C. (1984). *The Politics of Meaning: Power and Explanation in the Construction of Social Reality.* Tucson: University of Arizona Press.

Sennett, R. (1980). *Authority.* London: Secker and Warburg.

Sennett, R. (1986). *Palais Royal.* New York: Knopf.

Shaw, G.B. (1950). *The Doctor's Dilemma.* Harmondsworth: Penguin.

Simons, H.W. (1974). 'The Carrot and Stick as Handmaidens of Persuasion in Conflict Situations', in G. Miller and H. W. Simons (eds) *Perspectives on Communication in Social Conflict,* Englewood Cliffs, NJ: Prentice Hall.

Sims, H.P. Jr, Gioia, D.A. and associates (eds) (1986). *The Thinking Organization.* San Francisco: Jossey Bass.

Smith, J.L. (1973). *Melodrama.* London: Methuen.

Smith, K.K. and Berg, D.M. (1987). *Paradoxes of Group Life.* San Francisco: Jossey Bass.

Solomon, R.C. (1976). *The Passions: The Myth and Nature of Human Emotion.* Garden City, NY: Doubleday.

Srivastva, S. (ed.) (1983). *The Executive Mind: New Insights on Managerial Thought and Action.* San Francisco: Jossey Bass.

Srivastva, S. and associates (eds) (1986). *Executive Power.* San Francisco: Jossey Bass.

Starbuck, W.H. (1983). 'Organizations as Action Generators', *American Sociological Review* 48(1), 91–102.

Strauss, A. (1978). *Negotiations.* San Francisco: Jossey Bass.

Tichy, N.M. and Devanna, M.A. (1986). *The Transformational Leader.* New York: Wiley.

Weick, K. (1987). 'Perspectives on Action in Organizations', in J. Lorsch (ed.), *Handbook of Organizational Behavior,* Englewood Cliffs, NJ: Prentice-Hall.

Weinstein, E.A. and Deutschberger, P. (1963). 'Tasks, Bargains and Identities in Social Interaction', *Social Forces* 42(4), 451–6.

Whitaker, D.S. and Lieberman, M. (1964). *Psychotherapy and the Group Process.* New York: Atherton Press.

Woodman, R.W. and Sherwood, J.J. (1980). 'The Role of Team Development in Organizational Effectiveness: A Critical Review', *Psychological Bulletin* 88, 166–86.

Zijderveld, A.C. (1982). *Reality in a Looking Glass.* London: Routledge and Kegan Paul.